FRESNO CITY, CAL.

W Elliott & Co. for

S & SONS

ENTS.

11 PLANEING MILL	16 FRESNO WATER WORKS	
12 WINERY	17 FRESNO GAS WORKS	
13 CANNERY	18 EPISCOPAL CHURCH	
14 SCHOOL HOUSE	19 GRAND CENTRAL HOTEL (PROJECTED)	
15 ODD FELLOWS HALL	20 RAILROAD STATION	

Santa Clara
County
Free Library

REFERENCE

5816

Santa Clara County Free Library

California

HERITAGE FRESNÖ

HOMES AND PEOPLE

AMERICAN REVOLUTION BICENTENNIAL
1776-1976

Recognized by
Fresno Regional
Bicentennial
Commission

HERITAGE FRESNO

HOMES AND PEOPLE

122391
AMERICAN ASSOCIATION
OF UNIVERSITY WOMEN
FRESNO, CALIFORNIA • 1975

Library of Congress Catalogue Card No. 75-20772
ISBN 0-914330-06-3

First Printing, October 1975
Second Printing, December 1975

Published by
Historic Homes Committee
Fresno Branch
American Association of University Women
Produced by
Pioneer Publishing Co., Fresno

Manufactured in the United States of America

HISTORIC HOMES COMMITTEE

Fresno Branch
American Association of University Women

General Chairman	Valerie Comegys
Layout Chairman	Marge Belman
Research Chairman	Patricia Fey
Maps	Frances Trimble and Marty Freeburg
Title Page	Adele Huber
Secretary-Treasurer	Linda Stegmeir
Promotion	Bernice Hobe
Distribution	Rosellen Kershaw

COMMITTEE MEMBERS

Johanna Best	Adelaide Fisher	Ilene Marcum
Edith Brocks	Annidelle Flint	Viola May
Veda Devereux	Tomiko Ishikawa	Evelyn Moon
Doris Dillon	Helen Jensen	Fay Nowell
Joan Dinkin	Marian Jordan	Phyllis Wilson
Betty Ericson	Karen Kenefick	Naomi Young
	Joan Knapp	

Preface

Heritage Fresno Homes and People is a collection of architectural descriptions of historic homes in Fresno and seven surrounding communities and biographical sketches of the men and women who were first owners or best known occupants of the homes during the fifty years from 1872 to 1922.

For two years the Historic Homes Committee of the Fresno Branch of the American Association of University Women has engaged in a program of research and writing in order to produce this tribute to the Valley. We are honored that the Fresno Regional Committee of the American Revolution Bicentennial Committee has endorsed our project and has granted their logo for this book.

Criteria for selecting the ninety-three homes discussed in the following pages were as follows: The home had to be standing at the time of writing and had to be significant for reasons of age, architectural design, or civic contribution of the people who lived in the home. We are well aware that the list is not complete, and we regret that we could not include every home that meets these qualifications.

We believe, however, that we have compiled a unique architectural record that identifies for the first time noteworthy homes of Fresno and surrounding communities in Fresno County. The accompanying biographical sketches provide revealing details of our social and economic background.

We hope that this study will encourage Fresno County residents to preserve the historically significant buildings that have survived.

A systematic survey, undertaken by committee members who walked and drove through the streets, followed up by helpful suggestions from people interested in identifying and preserving our architectural heritage, produced a list of houses to be studied before including them in the book. The Department of Planning and Inspection of the City of Fresno relied in part on our work when they prepared a map of historic sites within the city limits of Fresno.

As the project proceeded, we turned first to documentary evidence concerning the history of the houses and their first owners. The record of land title transfers made available to us through the courtesy of officials at Safeco Title Insurance Company, when checked against names and addresses found in the various Fresno County and City Directories, helped to establish the date of construction and name of the first owner. Unfortunately, the records of the Tax Assessor's office either did not exist or were not available to us. Newspaper stories provided a source of information about houses, residential districts, and people. The County Department of Vital Statistics and the City Department of Planning and Inspection were sources of information. The books and scholarly articles that have been written about the city and county of Fresno were checked. Finally, we relied heavily on oral interviews and correspondence with men and women whose memories stretched back to the turn of the century. From them we gained many revealing glimpses of the social, economic and cultural life of an earlier generation in Fresno.

For architectural descriptions we received much help from architects Dennis Carner, who gave generously of his time and expertise; William Patnaude, who assisted early in the project; and James Nargis, who provided the description of the Meux House. We warmly acknowledge the assistance of these gentlemen.

We are most grateful for the generous assistance provided by Dr. Sam Suhler, History Librarian of Fresno County Library; Mabelle Selland, Executive Director of the Fresno County Historical Society;

continued

and C.W. Richard Atkins, William Bailey, Betty Kanawyer and Frances Cone of Safeco Title Insurance Company.

We are especially grateful to Rollin Pickford, who kindly permitted us to use his watercolor, *Each Spring Since 1893*, reproduced on the cover, and *The Twin Sisters*, reproduced on page 34; to Dorothy Stuart for her sketch of the Kearney Mansion; to Sarah Fey, who provided several sketches; and to Russell Fey, who gave his time generously in order to photograph most of the homes shown on the following pages.

The houses have been arranged by areas, beginning with the original boundaries of Fresno, incorporated in 1885, then in surrounding areas, and finally in seven adjacent communities. The accompanying maps make it possible to drive easily from location to location viewing the homes.

Additional copies of this book may
be obtained by writing to:
Heritage Fresno
American Association of University Women
2995 E. Buckingham Way
Fresno, California 93726

Introduction

In the fifty years from 1872 to 1922 the San Joaquin Valley was transformed from a dry plain devoted to sheep raising to verdant fields covered with crops, orchards and vineyards. Fresno grew in these years from a few sunbaked shacks to a city with a population between 45,000 and 50,000 in the center of the richest agricultural area of the world.

The railroad, irrigation, capital and hard work provide the keys to the story of Fresno and surrounding communities.

In 1871 Leland Stanford and other officials of the Central Pacific Railroad saw 2,000 acres of wheat growing on A.Y. Easterby's Banner Ranch. Lush and green, the grain had been irrigated by water brought from the Kings River by Moses Church. Impressed by the potential agricultural productivity of the area, Stanford selected the site, now Fresno, as a station on the new Central Pacific (Southern Pacific) Railroad pushing through the Valley. The stories of surrounding communities briefly told in the following pages are very similar.

Privately owned irrigation companies and then publicly controlled irrigation districts tapped the Kings River and San Joaquin River. As water from these sources drenched the Valley, people moved in, and the stock and wheat ranches were reduced to eighty-, forty- and twenty-acre tracts devoted to the more specialized and lucrative production of grapes and other fruits.

Capital was the third essential ingredient in the magnificent expansion of the Valley. The railroad, irrigation projects and accompanying land development required massive infusions of money. Only two examples from the complicated story can be offered. Moses Church, early-day sheep rancher and a well-known figure in the history of Fresno, organized the Fresno Canal and Irrigation Company. With inadequate capital, cursed by the financial depression of 1873 and expensive legal

problems, the company was taken over briefly by the Nevada Bank of San Francisco and finally by the Manchester Trust Company in Great Britain. English capitalists with their vast resources constructed many new canals and lateral ditches, straightened out legal entanglements and put the canal company on a firm business basis.

The second illustration involves land colonies, what today we would call "real estate developments," directed by men who had access to enough capital to cover the heavy initial expense of putting land into grapes and fruit. The Central California Colony, the first of these enterprises, offers an excellent example of the way the system worked. Bernard Marks, a man with ideas, contracted with William S. Chapman, a San Francisco promoter and speculator in land, for twenty-one square miles of land adjacent to Fresno. Chapman, in turn, was strongly backed by Isaac Friedlander, a wealthy grain merchant. They then subdivided six square miles into twenty-acre units, laid out avenues planted with trees, surveyed each lot to select the best place for irrigation ditches, constructed canal gates and even planted two-acre vineyards on each twenty acres. In 1875 they were vigorously advertising their land at $50 per acre. The twenty-acre tracts could be purchased for $100 cash; $12.50 per month for five years and $150 at the end of the fifth year. No interest was charged on any of the payments.

Hard work intelligently applied to the tasks confronting early settlers is possibly the most important theme in the story that unfolds in the first fifty years. Biographical sketches of Fulton G. Berry, who gave his first name to a Fresno street; J.C. Forkner, who developed the Fig Garden area, or Wylie Giffen, large-scale rancher and businessman, and the remaining ninety men and women discussed support the generalization.

The development of the city of Fresno paralleled

continued

that of the Valley. First came the railroad, around which clustered the first business houses and homes. Then in succession came the first public school, 1874; a volunteer fire company, 1875; the first church, 1876; the first policemen to help the marshal, 1885; gas and electric service, 1886; telephones, 1887; work on the sewer system began in 1889. The citizens had voted to incorporate in 1885, and by 1890 the population had reached 10,890.

The city of Fresno boomed in the late 1880's along with the rest of California, and languished during the depression of the early 1890's. Steady growth seems to characterize the period from 1900 to 1922 as city residences moved west on L Street and then north of Divisidero. This was a period, as the following pages show, in which enterprising men engaged in many different kinds of enterprise — real estate, lumber, oil, merchandising and, of course, agriculture.

In these years most of the homes included in this book were built — simple homes, such as the so-called Twin Sisters, identical houses built between 1900 and 1905 by William F. McVey for his daughters, and stately, elaborate mansions such as the Harvey Swift home, built in 1905 for the then enormous sum of between $35,000 and $50,000. All mark a portion of the Fresno story and stand today as visible reminders of the first fifty years of community building in the Valley.

Bobbye Temple

Table of Contents

Chapter One

ORIGINAL INCORPORATED AREA

Leland Stanford, inspired by the Easterby wheat fields, chose the site and a new city was born. When incorporated in 1885, Fresno was bounded by California, Angus, Divisadero and Tehama (Thorne) Avenues.

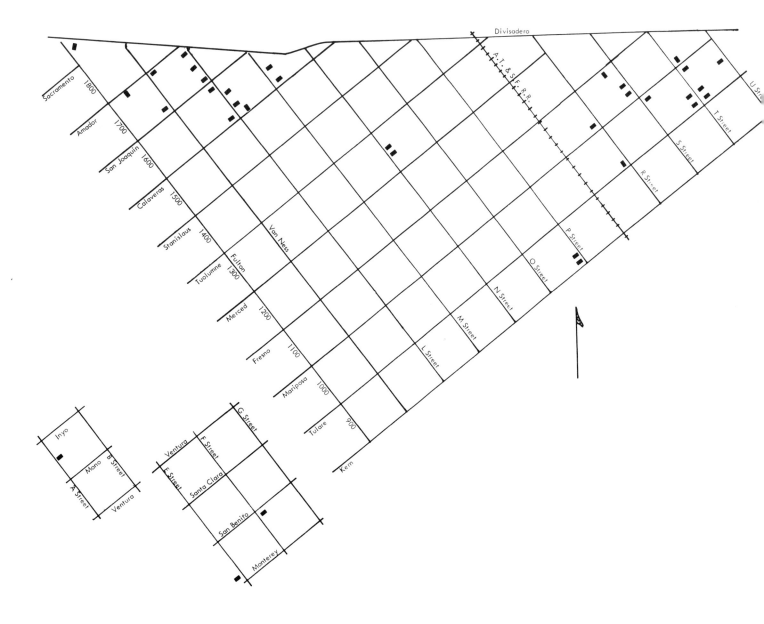

The Meux Home — 1007 R Street

Standing as a splendid symbol of Fresno's architectural tastes in her earliest days is a house whose life has nearly paralleled that of the city of Fresno. The beautiful Victorian at 1007 R Street, built by Dr. Thomas Richard Meux for his wife and three children in 1889, was continuously occupied by members of the family for eighty-one years until it was bought by the city of Fresno in 1970 to be restored to its original condition. The house has since been placed on the National Register of Historic places.

According to her grandson, Mrs. Meux sat down with the contractor and a book of house plans, and together "they put up a house." The plans of a one-story elaborate Victorian with cupola from the book of models became the second story of the new home and a first story was simply placed beneath the original design.

However impromptu the process of design may seem to us almost one hundred years later, the Meux house is of special historical significance as it is the finest example of Victorian construction in Fresno County today.

Carpenter artisans had an opportunity to exploit their craft in this era when a mixture of Queen Anne, Victorian Gothic, French Renaissance, Variegated Baroque and even a touch of Turkish and Italianate were used.

A wide veranda on two sides, which offers protection from the Valley sun, adds grace and elegance to the basic square structure. The windows have extending shutters opening from the bottom out, a feature unique to the Valley of this period. The double door entry with elegant stained glass enriches the approach which leads into a large entry with promenade staircase to the second floor.

The exterior walls feature three typical wood surfaces of the time. Horizontal clapboard provides a feeling of solidarity for both floors. The second floor is sheathed in fish-scales or scalloped shingles and a variegated pattern of shingles is to be found under the steeply-pitched gable roof. Other examples of wood carving can be seen in fan designs at the top of the pediment, the floral designs on the tower and the detailed roof trim. The upward thrust of the cupola on the left with its elaborate finial, gives a touch of the Victorian Gothic. The unique flaring of the chimneys is French Renaissance.

A stable, with storage room attached, is located on the site. Typical of those in the era in which the house was built, the stable includes stalls for horses, space to store the phaetons, surreys and a one-horse buggy.

Dr. Meux, born in Wesley, Haywood County, Tennessee, in 1838, attended the University of Virginia, and graduated from the University of Pennsylvania Medical School in 1860 at the age of twenty-two. In 1874, he married Mary Esther Davis in Brownsville, Tennessee, and they became the parents of John W., Mary D. and Anne Prenetta. Mrs. Meux was in poor health and on the advice of a brother, John P. Meux, who had moved to San Francisco in 1879, Dr. Meux decided to move his family to the Central Valley.

Property in a prime residential area of the city, at the corner of Tulare and R Streets, was purchased by the doctor from the County of Fresno as a home site in March, 1888, and the family moved into the house in January, 1889.

Establishing his medical practice in 1889, Dr. Meux served the community as a physician from his office and home the rest of his life. He served as president of the Fresno County Medical Society in 1896 and was described as a staunch member of the Fresno County Democratic Club and the Methodist Episcopal Church South.

Thomas Meux and his brother, John, owned vineyards in the county and he maintained an active interest in agricultural affairs.

Dr. Meux died at the age of ninety-one in 1929 and his daughter, Anne Prenetta Meux, died in 1970, having lived in the house since she was four years old. *The Fresno Bee* heralded this occupancy as establishing the longest individual residence in one of Fresno's oldest dwellings.

The Collins Home — 1107 R Street

The house at 1107 R Street, known as the "Collins house" which was completed in 1905, reflects a blend of styles. The exterior of channel siding has the corner boards of the Stick Style, and a frieze board under the roof. The columns, which have Ionic capitals, are plain, not fluted as is usually the case. The elaborate gingerbread in the gables reflects the Eastlake design. The prominent bay window on Mariposa Street has beautiful diamond-shaped leaded glass panes.

James D. Collins, the original owner, was proud of the fact that only clear pine was used in the construction of the house — "Not a knothole in it." The lumber was furnished by the Flume and Lumber Company, then owned by C.B. Shaver and Harvey Swift. The actual builder was a man named Dave Cowan.

Mr. Collins, a man of consequence in Fresno County for nearly fifty years, was born in Tennessee in 1843. After enlisting in the Confederate Army at the age of eighteen he was captured and spent three years in a Union prison. After the close of the war, he came west and settled in Fresno County in the Big Dry Creek area. Parents in the region lamented there being no school and supported Mr. Collins in the founding of an academy. The school was a half mile from a village which took the name "Academy." Mr. Collins taught school for many years as well as being a landholder. In 1876, he was elected to the California Assembly where he served a term and in 1898 was elected sheriff, and served for eight years. At the time of his death he had eight surviving children.

His son, Dr. Clinton Collins, the long time resident of the house, practiced medicine in Fresno until he was seventy-four. He served as president of the County Medical Society and in 1950 was elected president of the Community Hospital Staff. He had been on the board of directors of the Burnett Sanitarium, the hospital's parent institution.

Another son, William Collins, served as a Fresno County Supervisor for twenty-eight years, being elected to seven consecutive four year terms.

The Rehorn Home — 1050 S Street

Frank Rehorn, a widely-known local contractor and builder of commercial buildings, constructed only two residences in Fresno. One, his own beautiful home at 1050 S Street, was built of brick made from gray sand taken from the river at Antioch by the Golden State Brick Company in 1906. The other home, of red brick, he built for his friend, D.S. Ewing on T Street.

Built in the Georgian Colonial style, his house has an elaborate wooden portico supported by columns of brick as well as wooden columns which help to support the widow's walk. A hand-turned wooden balustrade surrounds the widow's walk. A magnificent hand-carved curving stairway dominates the spacious entry hall.

Born in New York City in 1862, Mr. Rehorn moved to Tennessee with his family when he was fourteen years old. At age nineteen he left home for Kansas where he learned the building trade, and in 1887 he came to California settling in Fresno. On November 24, 1890, he married Miss Myrtle Conrad.

The *Fresno Morning Republican* of December 15, 1914, reported that Mr. Rehorn presented the Chamber of Commerce with a cluster of grapefruit from a tree in his yard. The unusual cluster of five fruit measured an average of fourteen inches each in circumference. Sixty-one years later the tree is still bearing fruit.

The Republican Building, which he built at the corner of Tulare and Van Ness, now houses the McMahan's Furniture Store. He also built the Patterson Block and the old telephone building on Tulare Street.

After Mr. Rehorn's death, the family home was sold to H.H. Holland. In December 1941, it was bought by the Roman Catholic Bishop of Monterey Diocese. The Sisters of the Holy Cross, teachers at St. John's School, used it as a residence until the school closed. Since then there have been several owners.

The Aten Home — 1133 S Street

This California brown shingle home at 1133 S Street, constructed about 1914 by W.R. Ackerman for Mrs. C.B. Aten, continues to offer, after more than sixty years, comfortable residence for its owners. It reflects an indigenous California design pioneered by the famous Berkeley architect, Bernard Maybeck and the brothers Charles and Henry Greene of Pasadena, who sought comfortable dwellings that complemented the relaxed style of California living. A gabled roof over a deep porch provides shade and the generous overhanging eaves create attractive patterns of shade and light. Brown stained redwood inside and out characteristically converted these houses into cool dark caves during the hot day. By contrast the large windows on the second floor of this home could be opened up at night in order to provide comfortable sleeping accommodations.

Russell C. Fey

6

The Brix Home — 2844 Fresno Street

The elegant Italian Villa at 2844 Fresno Street, in use today as an office building, is unique in architectural design among Fresno's historic homes. Designed by the San Francisco architect Edward Foulkes, it represents one of the few homes of a true period design built in Fresno prior to World War I. A square tower set off-center, balustraded balconies, a slightly pitched roof, and the three varieties of attractive arches framing the windows add variety to the exterior and to the lengthy veranda or loggia across the front of the building. When constructed in 1911, the building was adjacent to thriving vineyards which, with the blue Sierra skies, made the attractive Italian Villa style most appropriate for its setting.

Herman H. Brix, who built the house in 1911, was born in Breslau, Germany in 1862. He came to Iowa after serving in the German army and later took up a homestead near Coalinga. From there, he went to Alaska during the gold rush, but returned in 1901 after hearing of the Blue Goose oil strike in the western part of the San Joaquin Valley.

His homestead, which he was unable to sell at any price to raise money for his trip to Alaska, he now sold for $820,000. It was said that he was a man ahead of his times. Even some of his friends were skeptical and thought him a dreamer, but his venture into the oil business proved them wrong. Having an inherent instinct for locating oil fields, he bought and sold a great deal of land in Coalinga for oil development. His first well was developed six miles from Coalinga by the Confidence Oil Company. Then, with a Mr. Bunting, he formed the B. and B. Oil Company. In 1903, with profits realized from selling land for oil development, he began investing in Fresno real estate. He built the Brix apartment building, and was a stockholder in, and construction engineer of, the Hotel Fresno—then the showplace of the Valley. His heirs later built the Brix office building.

The house has been designated a "Point of Historical Interest" by the Fresno County Board of Supervisors.

7

The Prescott Home — 2983 Tulare Street

F.K. Prescott, who had pioneered in Fresno's lumber business since 1883, built this magnificent home at 2983 Tulare Street in 1906. Following a predominantly Georgian Revival style, the house was built with the care of a knowledgeable lumberman plus expert craftmanship. The building originally had a beautiful wood interior. Boards of Black Sequoia specially milled near the General Grant Grove for this home were twenty-three feet long by eighteen inches wide. Clear pine with "no knots" was used in the dining room where there was also a splendid buffet twelve feet long, which has been moved to Key West, Florida by former owners. Finally, softly gleaming Brazilian mahogany graced the walls of the living room and entry hall.

For the exterior of his new home, Mr. Prescott, the successful lumberman, turned to brick and constructed walls three feet thick at the base, twenty-one inches at the second floor and nineteen inches at the third floor. Ceilings are ten and one-half feet high. Six wooden Ionic columns support the portico, and octagonal towers on each side of the entry reflect the design surmounted by elaborate dormers of Eastlake design.

Mr. and Mrs. Prescott, their baby son Edwin M. Prescott, and C.S. Pierce, the brother of Mrs. Prescott and business partner of Mr. Prescott, had come west from Iowa in search of a warmer and healthier climate. After a survey of other communities in northern California, they located permanently in Fresno and set up a lumber yard. The partners, Prescott and Pierce, contracted for the total output of a number of small logging operators in the Pine Ridge area, and with the assistance of Return Roberts, owner of the Madera Flume and Trading Company, prospered. In time Mr. Prescott organized the Valley Lumber Company which his sons, F. Dean Prescott and Edwin M. Prescott, continued to operate until 1958.

The house which Mr. Prescott built is presently in use as a mortuary.

The Martin Home —
1002 T Street

Listed for the first time in the 1914 City Directory, the house at 1002 T Street was probably built at this time. An expanded bungaloid home, it made use of large river rocks for fireplace and foundation. The arch over the porch and the lattice work are distinctive but not uncommon. The lattice work is a variation of the Western Stick Style.

George V. Martin, a lawyer and real estate man, was the first occupant of the house. He took title to the house in 1919 and then sold it to a Mr. Emirzian. Since 1960 it has been in use as a mortuary.

The Gundelfinger Home — 1020 T Street

Henry Gundelfinger, born in Michelbach, Germany in 1855, came to Fresno about 1880. His brothers, Louis and Leopold, also settled in the area, making Gundelfinger a name prominently associated with early day Fresno. Henry, a farmer, became a director of the Louis Einstein Company, a general store.

In 1891 Henry married Palmyre Raas, daughter of a socially prominent French family from San Francisco. Henry and his wife, a brilliant pianist, were active in civic affairs for many years. Palmyre was listed as a Christian Science Practitioner in the Fresno Directory of 1923.

In 1938, at the age of eighty-three, Henry returned to Germany. He brought back his sister, Clara Kahn, her son Emil, his wife and their two children, that they might escape Hitler's persecution of the Jews.

The 1020 T Street dwelling, which was the Gundelfinger's second home, was constructed in 1910 by E.J. Farr at a cost of $7,000. Unlike so many of Fresno's lovely older homes, this one has been saved from the bulldozer. Sold in 1972, the house has been restored for use as a private residence.

Russell C. Fey

The Ewing Home — 1025 T Street

D.S. Ewing, an attorney, chose his good friend, Frank Rehorn, to build the dignified brick home at 1025 T Street in 1916. Wide eaves cast a shadow over the second story windows. A wide porch extends across the full length of the house, and both porch and house roofs are tiled. The flat soffit under the eaves and repetition of the tile motif offers a pleasing variation.

The interior features were mahogany wainscoting and moldings, and coved ceiling in the living room. The upper walls and ceiling were finished with fabric pressed into wet plaster.

The house has offered almost continuous residence since the days of its construction, and the durable brick promises many more years of service and easy maintenance. In 1929 it was bought by Dr. J.H. Pettis.

A story to shock any meticulous housewife is told by Mrs. George Engstrom, who has lived in the house since she and her husband bought it in 1939. She recalls that at the end of May, just as the house was to change hands, Mrs. Pettis piled a great deal of trash in the fireplace and set fire to it, subsequently burning off most of the roof. Six weeks later, a contractor removed what vestiges of the roof remained, and the next day an unusual July rainstorm occurred. The deluge of water collecting in the second floor cascaded down the main staircase like Niagara Falls. Workmen brought in wheelbarrows of dirt and built dikes across the living room and dining room doors to channel the water out the front door.

Photograph c. 1907.

The Goodman Home — 1060 T Street

Gleaming white marble steps, since covered with concrete, once led to the spacious entry hall with crystal chandeliers and graceful hand carved winding stairway of the Georgian Colonial house at 1060 T Street.

Built in 1906 by Sol B. Goodman for his family, the house has finely grained wood siding and portico and dormer of classic, symmetrical proportions. Unusual is the balcony at the dormer, and the arched window. The four matched Ionic columns in front and pilasters at the corners of the house add dignity to its appearance. The house has five large fireplaces, one of which is in the spacious, well-lighted basement. His daughter, Ruth, recalls gala parties in the hospitable home, many of which were held in the basement.

Mr. Goodman, a native of Nashville, Tennessee, was a resident of California for seventy-five years until his death in 1924, and had been in the clothing business in Fresno for more than fifty years. Active in the project for widening Broadway and in modernizing the buildings along that street, he was known unofficially as "the mayor of Broadway."

After the 1906 San Francisco earthquake and fire, he traveled to the city to locate relatives who might have been without a place to live and brought them to stay with him in Fresno. A civic leader, he was a charter member of Temple Beth Israel and largely responsible for its construction. He also made available to war veterans the present Liberty Cemetery.

Before his death, Goodman expressed the wish that his ashes be scattered from Glacier Point, above the Yosemite Valley, but his daughter was not permitted to carry out the request.

The Hammond Home — 3005 Mariposa Street

This house at 3005 Mariposa Street built in 1912 by Thomas J. Hammond, reflects a blend of styles. The hipped roof and front dormer suggest the Georgian; however, the wide front porch which extends along the entire front of the house is a variation from the traditional. Perhaps most distinctive in this combination of styles are pillars of stone which support the porch without the usual pilasters.

Mr. Hammond is best remembered for his part in the last drive to get water transportation via the San Joaquin River from San Francisco Bay to Fresno, which received its chief impetus in the years between 1910 and 1915. The dramatic climax of this effort came in 1911 when a committee of citizens led by Mr. Hammond brought an excursion steamer from San Francisco Bay to Mendota. The gesture was designed to get political support for an appropriation of federal money to reshape the river for navigation purposes, including a means of surmounting the Miller and Lux dam at Mendota. A report to Congress by the United States Army Engineers that the river was more important for irrigation than for navigation, and the increasing importance of truck transportation on the state highways, ended the hopes for water transportation to Fresno.

Curiously, each of the four owners of this house has had a surname which began with letter "H."

The tall redwood tree in front was brought to Fresno as a seedling in a shoebox from the Santa Cruz mountains and planted by the young daughter of one of the owners.

The Meux Home — 1045 U Street

This large, comfortable frame home at 1045 U Street, distinguished by two prominent bay windows in front of the second floor, was built in 1907 as the first home of John W. and Edna Cooper Meux. Their marriage brought together two early Fresno families. Mrs. Meux's parents, Dr. and Mrs. John Cooper, had come to Fresno in the late 1870's, and Dr. Cooper was one of the original signers of the Fresno City Charter. John was the son of Dr. and Mrs. T.R. Meux who came to Fresno from Tennessee in 1888. He had grown up in the big house at Tulare and R Street and chose the location of his own home just four blocks away because it was on the edge of town where the quail hunting was good.

He was a rancher and land appraiser and died in 1952. Mrs. Meux lived in the home until her death in 1974.

Russell C. Fey

The Fassett Homes —
905 and 915 P Street

Two charming little homes that stand side by side at 905 and 915 P Street, which were built by B.A. Fassett around the turn of the century, reveal the opportunities for elaborate decoration when the builder also owned one of the three lumber yards in Fresno. In those days such businesses carried only lumber, moldings and turned wood decorations. They were the moderate cost homes of their day. One is said to have sold for $800 during the depression of the thirties.

The elaborate spool and spindle design on the porches and the balustrades around the porch were machine-made for lumber yards in this period and were used extensively to decorate these houses.

Mr. Fassett, a native of Maine and the son of Hanford's first judge, took full advantage of his opportunity to leave for us these two elaborately decorated Eastlake style homes.

Russell C. Fey

The Romain Home —
2055 San Joaquin Street

Built in 1905 for Mr. and Mrs. Frank Romain, this spacious home at 2055 San Joaquin Street where they lived for many years is in use today as a mortuary. The house is distinguished by an elaborate bay window. A long porch on two sides of the house supported by boxed pillars offers protection from the hot summers. Mr. Romain, for whom Romain playground is named, pioneered in Fresno's famous raisin industry. Born in Toronto, Canada, he worked first for the Canadian Pacific Railroad and then moved to Riverside, California, where he took charge of a packing plant. From there he moved to Fresno in 1887 in the midst of the economic boom of those years to establish a new packing plant for the Griffin and Skelly Company. In time he became District Manager for this thriving company which had become the California Packing Company.

Russell C. Fey

16

The Evinger Home — 2024 Amador Street

A residence unlike any other found in the search for Fresno's architectural heritage stands at 2024 Amador Street. Constructed in 1912, the building is unusual in two respects. First, it is one of the few brick houses constructed in old Fresno. Second, its three arches represent the Classical style, while the curvilinear facade, similar to that of the Alamo House just a block away represents one of the two examples of Mission Revival style in this book.

Simeon Evinger, the first owner, was listed in the Fresno City Directory of 1892 as a butcher and twelve years later as president of the Fresno Meat Company. By 1912 his occupation had become vineyardist. Subsequent residents included Mrs. Angelina Doherty, widow of William K. Doherty, a pioneer farmer who is said to have sown the first alfalfa crop in Kings County. In 1919 Bernard Goodman, manager of the Kinema Theatre, lived here.

The Davidson Home — 1762 Van Ness Avenue

Russell C. Fey

This beautiful colonial structure at 1762 Van Ness Avenue was designed and built in 1906 for Dr. and Mrs. Joseph Dobbins Davidson by J.R. Weirick. Predominantly Georgian Colonial with pediment windows on the first floor and squared ones on the second level, the house has a portico supported by tall Ionic columns. The roof of the portico was once surrounded by a balustrade. Dr. Davidson, who graduated from Vanderbilt Medical School in Nashville, Tennessee at age nineteen, came to Fresno in 1890. He entered into partnership with Dr. Deardorf, was appointed County Physician and became a specialist in modern surgical techniques. In 1901 he organized the Burnett Sanitarium, forerunner of Fresno Community Hospital, which was housed in a structure he built on Fresno Street. Dr. Davidson returned briefly to his native state in 1901 to marry Mrs. Louise Neal Peden of Nashville.

It is said that Dr. Davidson, pressed into emergency medical service during the 1906 San Francisco earthquake, ruined his hands and could never practice surgery again. In any event, failing health forced his early retirement several months before his death in 1908 at the age of forty-six. The Masonic funeral was held in the K Street (Van Ness) home, from which Dr. Davidson's body was shipped to San San Francisco for cremation, attended by Drs. J.L. Maupin, Trowbridge and Craycroft.

The next owner, Mr. Martin Luther Woy, came to Fresno from Clinton, Illinois in 1887, accompanied by his wife, Martha McCandless, and her twelve-year-old niece, Lula Penny. The party also included the A.V. Lisenbys and the O.J. Woodwards, who chartered a railroad car to move their household goods west with them.

One of Fresno's consistently successful businessmen, Martin Woy, operated the town's first livery business on J Street (Fulton). Later ventures included breeding and training fine pacers and trotters on his Easton ranch, farming in the American Colony and in Kern County. A real estate development partnership resulted in the subdivision of the Poppy Colony, and he also plotted the Wyhee Home tract. Mr. Woy was successfully involved in the development of the Coalinga oil fields.

Four years after his first wife's death in 1910, Mr. Woy married Miss Alice Kelly, and it was to this union that his only child, Martin Luther, Jr., was born.

Mr. Woy's civic activities included membership in the Sequoia Club, four year's service as chief of police, pound master, fire marshall, head of the volunteer fire department and leadership in the Chamber of Commerce.

He lived in the home from 1909 until his death in 1928, after which the home was leased for use as a mortuary. Upon Mrs. Woy's death in 1938, Mr. Dale Orr purchased the property which is still in use as a funeral home.

Russell C. Fey

The McWhirter Home — 1618 L Street

With an unsolved mystery in its past, this spacious home faces an uncertain future. Built about 1891, it was the home of Louis Bransford McWhirter and his wife, Nannie Blasingame McWhirter. Mrs. McWhirter was a member of one of the oldest and wealthiest families in the Fresno area. Her father, J.A. Blasingame, had located in Fresno County in 1857. Mr. McWhirter was a native of Kentucky and was associated with Vanderbilt University before coming to California. In 1884, he was appointed commissioner from Tennessee to the World's Fair in New Orleans. Impressed by the outstanding California exhibit, he eventually left Nashville for the Pacific Coast and from 1887 lived in Fresno. His marriage to Nannie Blasingame took place in 1889.

McWhirter practiced law for a short time, and then turned to newspaper work. He helped establish the *Daily Democrat*. In 1889 he moved to the editorial staff of the *Expositor*. He was a reform politician and became associated with the Bourbon wing of the Democratic Party. Through his efforts in 1891, a Democratic ticket was nominated in Fresno County, a first in the County's history.

A sweeping Democratic victory after a heated campaign may have led to the unsolved murder. On the night of August 18, 1892, McWhirter was ambushed and shot in his own yard at an early hour. The assassination was believed by most to be political and roused widespread interest and indignation. Newspapers all over the state carried the story.

Although a substantial reward of $25,000 was of-fered by the citizens of Fresno and the Blasingame family, it was never claimed. Two suspects were brought to trial. Although three trials were held, the juries were unable to reach a conviction for either suspect. There were many rumors that the murder was really suicide. McWhirter was known to be in serious financial difficulties and had taken out large insurance policies on his life. Lawyers for the defense promoted the suicide theory, but the widow was able to collect as there were no suicide clauses in the policies.

Mrs. McWhirter later remarried and members of the family lived in the home until 1910, when it was sold to Frank S. Granger. Mr. Granger was president and general manager of the Summit Lake Interurban Railway Company.

After 1917, the residents are listed as F.B. Fox and family. A daughter, Mary Elizabeth Fox Quibell, remembers growing up in the lovely old home.

The house is a large two-story structure with narrow clapboard siding. There is a wide porch extending across the front of the house with a balcony the same width above. Supported by large round pillars, both porch and balcony are decorated with spindle railings. The large windows are topped with arched leaded decoration which is repeated over the door. A boxed cornice on the roof is ornamented with dentils. A wide-screened porch stretches across the second floor in the rear.

The future of the home? . . . Like many of the former structures on this once fashionable L street address, it, too, may be razed for parking!

A magnificent Georgian Revival Style dwelling built in 1905 provided the home at 1605 L Street for Harvey Swift and the many guests whom he entertained at costume balls, birthday parties and church affairs in 1905 and the years following. Quality construction coupled with attention to small detail gives timeless beauty to this house.

On a brick foundation the house rises two and one-half stories to a roof broken by a dormer to provide a tasteful balance. Decorative brackets with a frieze run horizontally with the roof lines. An open portico, with six Ionic columns thirty feet in height which support the roof, offers an impressive approach to the front doorway, which is flanked on either side by windows with beveled and leaded glass. Above the entryway at the second story level is a balcony surrounded by a balustrade supported by two more Ionic columns of lesser height on each side of the front door. Four French doors flanked by triple sash windows, leaded and beveled, lead into the interior at the second story. Within, spacious rooms, three brick fireplaces and a stairway with solid railing add to the beauty of this old house. A ballroom in the basement adds the last touch for the generous entertaining of the pre-World War I period.

The house, constructed by Harvey Swift, is a symbol of his success as a lumberman. The cost was estimated to be between $35,000 and $50,000. A native of New York, he moved first to Michigan and then to California, where with his brother he organized the Fresno Flume and Irrigation Company. In due time he bought out his brother and along with C.B. Shaver expanded the business, which upon Shaver's death was re-named Fresno Flume and Lumber Company. He was also active for a time in the developing oil industry in the Valley and was a large stock holder in the Hicks-Hoffman Navigation Company. A member of many community organizations, he helped promote the district fair and supported the Y.W.C.A.

Beveled Glass entry panel.   Russell C. Fey

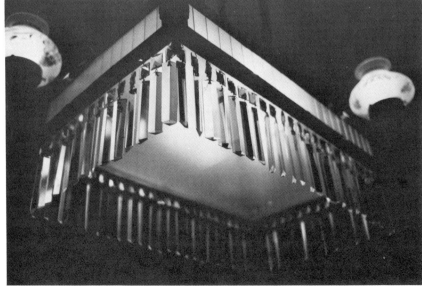

Original dining room light fixture.   Russell C. Fey

20

Russell C. Fey

The Swift Home —
1605 L Street

Photograph c. 1930.

Courtesy Lisle Funeral Home

21

The Thomas Home — 1642 L Street

This handsome square two-story house at 1642 L Street was built in the 1890's by Dr. Montgomery Thomas, a dentist who gave up his practice to become a real estate developer.

Here he and his bride, the former Agnes Helm, made their home on the tree-lined street near relatives and friends.

Shingles, popular in this period, cover the exterior of the house, which is basically Georgian in design with a prominent portico. Its asymmetrical appearance may be due to the fact that there was a change of builders during the four years it was under construction. A large front door, flanked by leaded windows on either side and surmounted by a Palladian window, reveals the attention given to the entrance where guests in those days of elaborate entertaining were first received. Most unusual architectural feature is the imposing semi-circular bay to the right of the front door with a rounded leaded window above it on the second floor.

Dr. Thomas, a native of Sedalia, Missouri, came to Fresno in 1885 and attended the old White Grammar School at N and Fresno Streets. In 1892, he was graduated from Fresno High School with the school's second graduating class, and four years later graduated from the University of California School of Dentistry.

22

The trees and quiet shade surrounding this old home at 1651 L Street suggest the more leisurely pace at the turn of the century, although the house has been extensively remodelled. In addition, the home commemorates the memory of William J. Dickey, a genial and civic-minded man for whom Dickey Playground was named.

In 1901 Alfred Kutner, formerly of Kutner, Goldstein & Company, a hardware store, but later Vice-President and Manager of the Farmers National Bank, built the house. Three years later, in 1904, Kutner sold the home to Dickey who had come west from Ohio

The Kutner Home — 1651 L Street

and settled in Fresno by 1880. Engaging in a variety of businesses, Mr. Dickey clerked for Kutner and Goldstein, was desk clerk at the Morrow House, wrote insurance, invested in the First National Bank and the People's Savings Bank and dabbled in wool and real estate. Land that he had purchased in the Coalinga area at a tax delinquent sale paid off handsomely during the oil boom.

He died in 1912, at the age of fifty-nine, leaving $25,000 for public purposes. The sum of $10,000 was bequeathed to the City of Fresno to purchase apparatus for the children's playgrounds; $5,000 went to the Fresno County Humane Society, and the income from the remaining $10,000 supports a scholarship for a deserving student.

During the late 1920's a Mrs. Rudy operated a tearoom in this home. About 1933 Dr. and Mrs. Frank MacCracken, both osteopathic physicians, bought the property from Mrs. Stockdale, a sister of Mrs. Rudy. They remodelled it extensively to serve as home and medical offices. They lived at this location for twenty-nine years until the house was sold to the current owners.

The Gundelfinger Home — 2201 Calaveras Street

The Louis Gundelfinger home at 2201 Calaveras Street was built in 1912 according to the design of a San Francisco architect, Edward T. Foulkes. It is an adaptation from a classical style sometimes described as High Victorian Italianate or English Roman style as evidenced by the treatment of the lower windows, arched in the upper third part; the keystone bisecting the top part of the window casement on the second floor and the prominent brackets under the eaves. Certainly this magnificent dwelling, now used as a home for the retired elderly, was a fitting reward for years of work as merchant and civic leader of Fresno.

Born in Germany, Louis Gundelfinger, one of three brothers who have contributed to the Fresno story, came to San Francisco in 1868 and worked as bookkeeper for Levi Strauss, famous for his "Levis." When a boyhood friend, Louis Einstein, needed assistance at his store he persuaded Mr. Gundelfinger to move to Fresno in 1877. In time he became manager and then president as well as part owner of the pioneer mercantile firm of Einstein and Company. Later he helped to found the Bank of Central California. All in all, his career reveals business competence combined with an interest in the cultural improvement of Fresno. He was director of the Fresno Art Association, member of the commission in charge of Roeding Park, and instrumental in the organization of the Fresno Traffic Association which sought more equitable railroad rates at the turn of the century.

Photograph c. 1915.

Courtesy Fresno County Historical Society

L Street — Past and Present

Russell C. Fey

The Bean Home — 1705 L Street

In 1897 William A. Bean bought two lots at a sheriff's sale for two hundred dollars. Before 1900 he had built this house at 1705 L Street — a narrow clapboard structure with a narrow porch across the front. Elaborately incised, decorative detail distinguishes this old home with pilasters that rise on each corner of the home. The same design is continued on the wooden columns supporting the porch, the corner posts of the balustrade, and the pilasters found on both sides of the front door. An oval window to the right of the front door provides another unusual detail. A distinctive decoration is to be seen in the entablature of the porch.

A hitching post on the Calaveras side of the home is the subject of a painting by Rollin Pickford, a Fresno artist.

All in all, the house presents a rather formal appearance where Mrs. Bean, rumored to have been "quite a social person," could receive her guests in a dignified setting.

The Long Home — 1727 L Street
(later The Black Home)

The imposing red brick house at 1727 L Street has a large portico supported by Ionic columns. Above the portico is a widow's walk surrounded by a balustrade. Dormers decorated with shingles in fish-scale design flank the pediment in the center of the house, which in turn is broken with three windows, the center one surmounted by an oval light. A porte-cochere on the north side sheltered the carriages which swept up to the home. A large carriage house which contained living quarters is in the rear.

Two well-known business men and their families have lived in this house. Arthur B. Long, vice president of the Fresno Flume and Irrigation Company, acquired the house in 1907. The flume, which carried lumber from the Shaver Lake area to the valley, was considered "one of the greatest enterprises ever established in Fresno County."

The house was occupied by the Long family until the death of Mr. Long and then was sold to the Fred P. Black family, for whom it is best known. A veteran Fresno merchant, Mr. Black built a retail grocery empire and helped to revolutionize the grocery trade in California with one of the first cash and carry grocery stores.

Black, who was born in London, Ontario, Canada, came to San Jose with his family as a boy in 1877. When he came to Fresno in 1913, grocery stores delivered their products by horse and wagon. The larger stores had as many as 100 horses and made three or four deliveries daily in almost every section of town.

An earlier change that he inaugurated in the food business was that of packaging in convenient amounts staples which ordinarily sold in bulk. These products included beans, rice, potatoes, crackers, cookies and candy.

At the time of his death in 1949, Black owned five grocery stores in Fresno and ten in Stockton.

The Helm Home — 1749 L Street

The Frank Helm home at 1749 L Street, known as the Alamo House was built in 1901-2 though his father, William Helm, acquired the land in 1890. It offers one of the few examples of Mission style architecture in the Valley. The distinctive, elaborate front design is similar to the famous building in Texas. The Moorish detail of point and round, the quatrefoil or star-shaped window, and balcony of wrought iron strap work also suggest the old Texas Mission. William Helm, a grandson who grew up in the house, vividly remembers experiencing the tremors from the 1906 San Francisco earthquake in the house.

One of the many substantial homes that were constructed on L Street at the turn of the century, it attracted the attention of M. Theo. Kearney, the famous land developer, who published a picture of the home in a promotional brochure sent out in 1903 to prospective buyers of twenty-acre irrigated tracts, referring to it as a "typical Fresno residence."

William Helm, the founder of the family long identified with Fresno County, was born in Canada, and in 1859, at age nineteen, took passage to California via New York and Panama. By 1865, he had acquired herds of sheep which he brought to the Dry Creek section, six miles northeast of the present site of Fresno, when the area was only a windswept plain. His winter quarters were on the site of the present Court House.

He bought 2,640 acres of land from William Chapman at a cost of a dollar an acre, and gradually increased his holdings to 16,000 acres of land and 22,000 head of sheep. For many years he was considered the largest sheep rancher in California.

Mr. Helm, who built the Gould Ditch and the Helm Building, located at Fulton and Fresno Streets, also built homes for each of his seven children, two of which still stand on L Street. His own home and those of two of his daughters on Fresno Street were torn down when the Fresno Community Hospital expanded.

28

The County Hospital 350 feet by 250 feet about completed, and two "typical homes in Fresno" in 1903 according to a promotional brochure published by M. Theo Kearney. House on the right is obviously the Helm home.

Doorway detail.

The Einstein Home — 1600 M Street

This massive house at 1600 M Street, whose most prominent feature is the roof, was designed to cope with the intense Valley heat in the days before air-conditioning. The English thatch motif, revealed in the rounded and undulated eaves dominating the roof, recalls the thatching so prominent in rural England.

The relatively small windows gathered in groups are set back in the double width walls, which are built with two rows of bricks providing an insulating air space between. The house had a "morning room" upstairs with an eastern exposure, a summer parlor in the basement, and a third floor ballroom.

Designed by Edward T. Foulkes, a San Francisco architect, the house was built by Hans Hansen, a Fresno builder. The building permit issued December 12, 1912, was for $28,500. A permit for the garage for $1450 was issued in 1913.

This location was chosen by Louis Einstein and his wife Eda for their family home so that he could continue to walk to his business downtown. His earlier home on Fresno's "Nob Hill" was situated on K Street (now Van Ness) on the site of the present Hardy Theater.

A pioneer merchant and banker in Fresno, Mr. Einstein was born in Germany and came to America at the age of eighteen. At the invitation of a relative, he came to the growing city of San Francisco to work as a bookkeeper and in January, 1871, came to the San Joaquin Valley where he was a partner in a store dealing in "grain, flour and provisions" in Visalia.

In June 1874, not long after the vote to move the county seat from Millerton to the new railroad town of Fresno, the Visalia firm bought the early-day firm of Otto Froelich, and Mr. Einstein moved to Fresno.

He was founder and president of the Bank of

Central California, which was organized in 1887, and had extensive business and residential real estate holdings. Before the bank was organized, he had financed the grain, sheep and cattle ranchers during the dry farming era and often carried their accounts until a good season, when the total accumulated debt could be wiped out.

Ben Walker, in the Fresno County Blue Book, says many a tale has been told of this quiet, retiring man's financial aid given at times on no more than his faith in the integrity of the applicant.

As a public service, beginning on July 1, 1881, the Louis Einstein Company kept a rain gauge, and this was continued until 1887 when the Government station was established. Mr. Einstein helped in organizing the free library movement, was a patron of the liberal arts and music, and took an active interest in the formation of the Unitarian Church of Fresno.

The Y.W.C.A. bought the house for use as their Activities Building in 1950. They transferred their offices to the 1600 M Street location, where it has been used as their organization headquarters and for all types of cultural and educational activities as well as social events for the past twenty-five years.

This building has been designated a "Point of Historical Interest" in Fresno County by the County Board of Supervisors.

The Y.W.C.A. Residence — 1660 M Street

The Y.W.C.A. Residence at 1660 M Street was designed by Julia Morgan and built in 1922. It is located next door to the Activities Building and has given more than fifty years of continuous service in providing housing for young women in Fresno County.

Julia Morgan was one of the foremost women architects in California. She was the first woman architect to be licensed in California. Born in San Francisco in 1872, she was the first woman to be graduated in Engineering from the University of California, in 1894, and the first woman to receive a Master's Degree from the Beaux Arts in Paris, where she also studied Architecture. After her return from Paris, Miss Morgan studied with Bernard Maybeck, the architect who had a tremendous influence on design in California.

Opening her own office in San Francisco, Miss Morgan designed more than 700 public buildings and private residences and was for many years the official architect of the Y.W.C.A. in the West. She built residences in Honolulu, Pasadena, Long Beach, and Oakland, as well as Fresno. She is perhaps best known for her design of the spectacular estate at San Simeon, popularly known as the Hearst Castle.

Deliberately adapted to Fresno's climate, this harmoniously designed building had great care given to the function for which it was constructed. The exterior might best be described as an adaptation of the Italian Villa style: low-pitched hip roof, smooth, stucco wall surfaces, and broad low-walled, unroofed front veranda. Windows are of two types, arched and rectangular, with the arches reflecting the Romanesque style. Shallow balconies, with simple wrought iron railings and supports, under the second floor windows are characteristic of the style.

In other respects the design meets the need for pleasant living conditions for the young women by creating an inner courtyard where privacy may be obtained out-of-doors. The sleeping porches at the rear of the third floor wings were especially adapted for Fresno's summer climate. Once screened, they have now been enclosed so that they can be used all year.

The interior has a lounge for the residents, a small library, and a spacious recreation hall which has recently been redecorated so that it can be used by volunteer workers to provide lunches to large groups as an additional source of funds for the organization.

This building has been designated a "Point of Historical Interest" by the County Board of Supervisors.

The Graff Home — 916 Divisadero

Hans Graff, a native of Denmark, came to Fresno in 1886 and worked in the grocery department of Louis Einstein and Company. Four years later he started his own store, which rapidly expanded until he located at Kern and Van Ness with a complete line of groceries, hardware, and crockery. By the turn of the century he was the largest dealer in groceries in this part of the state. He introduced the co-op system so his clerks could acquire an interest in the company.

The Graffs first moved to a small house on this lot in 1894 when this section of Divisadero was known as Nielsen Avenue. After three children were born, the small house was moved east near M Street while the present large house was constructed on the lot in 1905. When the Graffs moved into their new home a Danish artist, Marius Schmitt, lived with them for six months, doing paintings on the walls of the living room, dining room and library. The Dr. L.N. Pearson family, later residents, recall the beautiful fresco of roses and leaves painted on the ceiling of the living room with leaves trailing down the walls. The work remained until the house was redecorated in 1948. Hans Graff had a very important influence on the early years of Fresno both as a merchant and as director of the Danish Creamery Association. the California Associated Raisin Company, the Fresno Building and Loan Company and as a trustee of the Fresno State Normal School.

This imposing home appears to the passerby very much as it did when it was first constructed. The elegant capitals on the large columns are a composite of Ionic and Corinthian style. The roof is supported by a boxed cornice with frieze and brackets. The effect of a Palladian window is given by the beveled glass fan over the living room window. After use through the years as a boarding house and a doctor's office, the building has taken a new lease on life as a wedding and reception center. The interior has been extensively remodeled for its current use, but the classical Greek Revival exterior is unchanged.

The Twin Sisters, a painting by Rollin Pickford of the McVey homes. (Reproduced by permission).

Courtesy *Fresno Bee*

The McVey Homes — 1322 and 1326 N Street

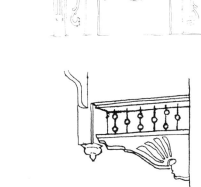

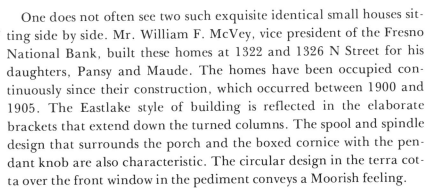

One does not often see two such exquisite identical small houses sitting side by side. Mr. William F. McVey, vice president of the Fresno National Bank, built these homes at 1322 and 1326 N Street for his daughters, Pansy and Maude. The homes have been occupied continuously since their construction, which occurred between 1900 and 1905. The Eastlake style of building is reflected in the elaborate brackets that extend down the turned columns. The spool and spindle design that surrounds the porch and the boxed cornice with the pendant knob are also characteristic. The circular design in the terra cotta over the front window in the pediment conveys a Moorish feeling.

The house at 1326 N Street was purchased by John Kurtovich, a restaurant owner, in 1923 for $6,500. Mr. Kurtovich had come to San Francisco from Yugoslavia in 1905, but the 1906 earthquake convinced him that he should move inland and he came to Fresno. In 1920 he returned to Yugoslovia and brought back his bride, Mary. Mr. and Mrs. Kurtovich continue to reside in the home. He purchased the 1322 N Street house in 1961 from Mrs. Augusta Johannsen, who had lived there since 1905.

The Okonogi Home — 746 A Street

Constructed prior to 1914, this home at 746 A Street was the residence of Dr. Bunkuro Okonogi and his family after he purchased it around 1920.

Remembered as one of the most respected and beloved members of Fresno's Japanese community, Dr. Okonogi, born in 1872 in Fukushima, Japan, was the ninth son of a doctor. Having attended medical school in Tokyo, Dr. Okonogi came to Fresno in the 1890's to serve the area's Japanese community. He started his first hospital in 1901 in a frame building at 736 E Street.

Twenty-five years later he built a thirty-eight room, full service brick hospital at 708 E Street on the corner of Mono, site of the present-day Danish Creamery. Known as the Okonogi Sanitarium, the hospital ministered to the sick of all races.

In 1902 Dr. Okonogi married Kiko Akiyama, a second-generation Japanese-American of Menlo Park, California. During the years before World War II Dr. Okonogi served a term as president of the Japanese Association of Fresno and was president of the now defunct Industrial Bank of Fresno.

With the onset of World War II, the entire Okonogi Sanitarium was moved to the Pinedale Assembly Center. Included with other personnel was Dr. Hugo Okonogi, the doctor's son who had joined him in his Fresno practice. Mrs. Okonogi had died at the age of fifty-six in 1936, but their daughter Ena was also sent to the Pinedale Center. In time Dr. Hugo was sent to the Merced Assembly Center to render badly needed medical services there. From this assignment he volunteered for military service and joined other native Americans of Japanese descent in the 442nd Infantry, a combat team which served out the course of the war in the European theatre. The elder Dr. Okonogi and Ena went from Pinedale to internment at Poston, Arizona Camp II, where he remained in practice as camp physician until the war ended. Ena was subsequently relocated to a Boston internment camp.

Following the war, Dr. Okonogi returned to Fresno to practice for a few years until his illness and death in 1950 at the age of seventy-eight. True to his humanitarian spirit, he provided in his will that all debts of his patients be cancelled.

Dr. Hugo remained in the U.S. Army as a career officer and now lives in retirement at Wellfleet, Massachusetts. Ena, a graduate of Illinois Woman's College who had done two years of graduate work at Wellesley, returned to Fresno and worked in the Fresno State College Library. Now Mrs. Ena Okonogi Sakamoto, she still resides in Fresno.

The white frame house on A Street remains much the same, located in a residential neighborhood of tree-lined streets, around the corner from the neighborhood school and across the street from a city playground.

36

With its vertical lines, high steep roof and exposed framing, this house at 305 E Street stands as an excellent example of the Stick style of architecture. Not only does it represent an unusually pure version of a well known American architectural style of the nineteenth century, but it stands as a present day symbol of the Volga Germans who left Czarist Russian for freedom in America.

German-Russians were early attracted to our fertile valley, and many settled in Fresno's old "German Town" on the west side of the Southern Pacific tracks. As rapidly as they accumulated capital, they bought farm land and farmed as they had for so many years in the "old country."

One of these early German settlers was the Reverend Jacob Legler, organizer of the Cross Lutheran Church. He bought two lots on E Street in September of 1899. He persuaded his nephew, Carl Legler, who was a school teacher among the Germans on the Volga River, to come to Fresno. Carl had already been influenced by literature he had received from Fresno land promoters so he brought his large family to Fresno in 1902. They settled into and enlarged the home built on the property owned by his uncle.

Carl, with his educational background, found it easy to become a minister and as the Reverend Carl Legler, he served the Saint Paul's Lutheran Church on California Avenue for many years.

The house still remains in the family and is now occupied by Leopold Legler.

The Legler Home — 305 E Street

Marge Belman

Russell C. Fey

The Vartanian Home — 362 F Street

Considered to be the oldest home in Fresno west of the Southern Pacific tracks, the Henry Vartanian home at 362 F Street is of unusual interest not only because of its architectural style but also because a complex of buildings — barn, water tank and outhouse — have survived to provide a graphic illustration of the living style of the 1890's.

In the days before Fresno had municipal water

service, a well, windmill and a water tower of sufficient height to provide adequate pressure at the faucets were necessities. The windmill has vanished, but the tower remains. Within its framework and under the tank was the coolest spot on the place and a good place to sleep on the hot summer nights.

First owner was Howvageem (Henry) Vartanian, who in the 1890's had a jewelry store where the Fresno Hotel is now located and for whom this building was constructed about 1894. Here he raised five children.

Built on a sturdy brick foundation with full basement, the original home had fourteen foot ceilings and three bedrooms. As the family grew, so did the house, and an additional bedroom was added some years later. This house is essentially Stick style with a number of variations common in the

1890's. The siding is one inch by eight inch redwood shiplap, but shingles in fish scale design provide a variation in the gable which is broken by a U shaped aperture. A prominent bay window decorated with colored glass insets is a customary feature of the time. There was disagreement about the building of the bay window; Vartanian fired the first builder, and another man finished the job. Most distinctive perhaps is the wooden frieze around the top of the porch and the elaborate scroll work to be seen in the gable. The sturdy balustrade around the bottom of the porch provides a conventional Eastlake touch.

The Vartanian family home also bears witness to the distinctive contribution of the Armenian people who have given such a flair to the Fresno story. As early as 1881 the Seropian brothers had arrived by train and in time had established a fruit packing plant. Early Armenian settlers introduced figs and melons from the Middle East and turned readily to business. By 1918 it is estimated that there were about 4,000 Armenians in Fresno and surrounding areas, drawn here by letters from the first arrivals.

One of the best known members of the Vartanian family is Jack, who made his boxing debut in 1919. In 1923, fighting under the name "Jack Powell," he won the welterweight championship of California. He is included in the Fresno Boxing Hall of Fame. He and other fighters of the 1920's trained in the barn, which still stands.

The prestigious portion of Fresno as shown on a lithograph of 1891 was north of the Southern Pacific between Divisadero and Tuolumne.

Opportunity! c. 1919.

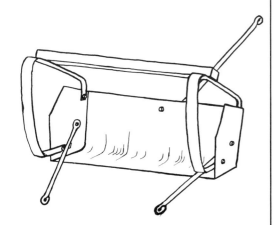

The famous Fresno Scraper.

40

Chapter Two

THE TOWN MOVES NORTH AND EAST

As transportation improved with trolley lines
(horse-drawn in 1888 and electric in 1902) and
new streets, people began to move beyond the
city limits.

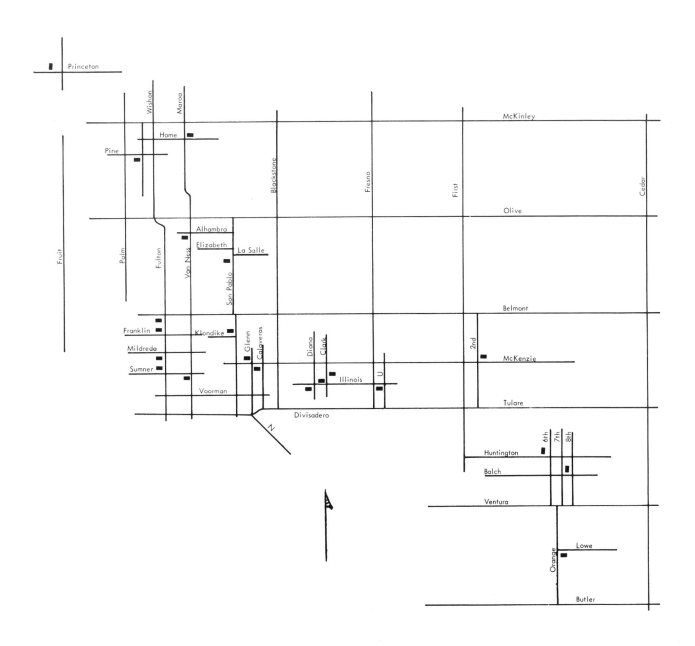

The McAlpine Home — 171 North Van Ness Avenue

Alexander McAlpine was a station agent for the railroad in Colorado and also conducted a very profitable business in buying and selling cattle. In April of 1900, he, his wife and seven children were taking a train trip through the San Joaquin Valley when they stopped in Fresno. He was so taken with the blossoming trees, the new shoots just bursting forth on the vines and the distant mountains, that he decided this was where he wanted to live.

He retired at forty-one and moved his family to Fresno where he bought the home at 171 N. Van Ness which had been completed just three months previously by a Mr. Crawford. It was an attractive redwood frame home with curving veranda on two sides and fish scale shingle detail in the gables. Three years later he paid an artist $2,500 to paint the woodwork all through the house with a false grain to resemble oak, which he had long desired. This was an artform of the time and consisted of a basecoat topped by a glaze which was artfully scored with a comb and the fingertips to resemble the grain of oak. The work was so excellent that even today the interior doors and woodwork appear as fresh and new as the day they were done. Part of a citrus orchard had to be removed to make room for the house and some of these original trees are still producing on the property.

Mr. McAlpine acquired the land east of Van Ness and from Belmont to Divisadero and subdivided it into lots. When asked later why he had made the streets of College, Park and Nevada so narrow, he replied that buggies were narrow and much travel was still by horseback which didn't require much width.

The home was acquired by Mr. McAlpine's grandaughter and her husband, H. Wayne Taul, in 1946. He has used it as an office for his engineering business ever since.

The Alexander Home — 235 North Fulton Street

This beautiful home at 235 North Fulton was built in 1908 or 1909 for Hugh H. Alexander, an early day Fresno real estate man who operated the Alexander Land Company.

The Ionic columns which reach up three stories in height and the pediment which reflect the Classical Revival style are first to catch the eye, and the intermediate balcony provided a pleasant place to sit to catch the breeze or to take afternoon tea.

Born in Scotland, Mr. Alexander came to Fresno in 1894 and lived here until his death in 1936 at the age of eighty. His wife, Harriet, who lived until 1947 was born in Nova Scotia. The Alexanders lived at 235 North Fulton Street until 1926 at which time they moved to smaller quarters.

Subsequently the house was occupied by several owners, including Flair of Fresno and, finally, in 1970 it became the Artefactorage.

Russell C. Fey

The Farr Home — 245 North Fulton Street

Elmer Jewett Farr, a contractor, built this home at 245 North Fulton for his family residence soon after buying the property in 1907. Of rather austere design, the second floor is fully shingled and the first floor is covered with narrow shiplap. The porch extends across the front of the house, but has a roof only over the entry. Two columns of Doric design and two pilasters support the porch.

Farr, who was born in New York in 1862, came to California in 1897 with his wife and two children. Although his first employment in Fresno was with the railroad, Farr soon became involved with construction, a vocation which left a lasting impression on the architectural face of Fresno. Many of the homes on Van Ness Avenue were built by Farr, and for a number of years he was in charge of building operations for the Fresno City Schools. He is best known for the construction of Roosevelt High School.

When Mr. Farr located his home on North Fulton, it was known as Forthcamp Avenue. A street car from town ran past the Farr's front door to the end of the line at Belmont several blocks to the north.

Active in civic affairs, Farr was the first president of Fresno's Contractors Association, which later became the Fresno Builders Exchange. He and his wife, Carrie, planned to observe their golden wedding anniversary in October 1940, but his death on May 17th of that year prevented this joyous celebration.

The house is now used as the Garden House Tea Room.

Russell C. Fey

The Proffitt Home — 405 North Fulton Street

John William Proffitt, born in Tennessee, spent most of his life in Graham, Young County, Texas, engaged in cattle raising. While there he was well acquainted with John Lisle, Jake Mittenthal and George Levin Aynesworth, all of whom subsequently settled in Fresno. Mr. Lisle founded the Lisle Funeral Home; Mr. Aynesworth practiced law and Mr. Mittenthal operated a shoe store in the growing community.

In 1907 Mr. Proffitt, then in his sixties, sold his cattle interests and came to Fresno County. He and his wife had a large family, four daughters and three sons, and with their help he planned to become a citrus grower in Sanger and, as the husband of one of his granddaughters writes, rule over them like a "chieftain." He made an initial deposit of $250,000 in a bank at Sanger, thereby establishing himself as a substantial citizen. Business matters brought him to Fresno frequently, and he became interested in the suburbs just north of Divisidero where the fine homes of many prominent families were being built. He purchased from Mr. Forthcamp, six twenty-five foot lots running north from the corner of Franklin and Forthcamp Avenue (North Fulton Street).

In 1911 he erected this two story, six bedroom frame house on the four lots nearest the corner. The remaining two lots were used for garden and orchard and an iron fence that still remains enclosed the entire property. The house is predominantly Queen Anne style with some interesting architectural features. The cupola over the porch,

held down to the first story level, offers a contrast to the straight gable roofs. Similarly the curvilinear balcony with shingles contrasts with the clapboards in the pediment. Notice the capping on the chimney.

Mr. Proffitt was seldom willing to compromise. Family members have many such anecdotes which go far to disclose his personality.

One of these concerns the occasion of a divergence of viewpoint between himself and the then Farmers and Merchants National Bank. As a result of their failure to achieve detente, Proffitt demanded withdrawal of the entire sum of his deposits, immediately and in gold coin. After some remonstrance the bank complied, to the extent of a weight that he was, of course, unable to budge. He importuned the bank officials to maintain custody whilst he arranged transportation, but they declined, leaving him no alternative to swallowing what pride he had left and returning the coins to deposit. This is said to be the only time Proffitt ever surrendered a point.

After his wife died in 1912 Mr. Proffitt abandoned his plans for a citrus ranch. (His sons and daughters and their spouses had not always agreed with his plans.) He retired to the big house with a spinster daughter, Ida, and an infant granddaughter of his deceased daughter, Rose. In 1913 when another daughter, Minnie, was left a widow in Texas, he sacrificed the garden and orchard to build a small house for her and her three children. Mr. Proffitt died in 1925, but Miss Ida continued to live in this home until her death in 1960 at age eighty-four.

45

Russell C. Fey

The Cobb Home — 437 North Fulton Street

The large two story house constructed in 1913 at 437 North Fulton was the home of Charles H. Cobb, the second man to enter the automobile business in Fresno. He and his brother had a livery stable in the Armory Theater Building, now the site of the Gottschalk's downtown store, but in progressive fashion he turned to automobile sales in 1907. Prominently identified with many civic enterprises, he was first president of the Fresno Auto Dealers Association, board member of Chapman College and state senator (Democrat) for the 1926-1930 legislative term.

His home is unusual in that three Ionic columns rather than matched pairs rise to the roof. A deep porch at the second story offers shade and a view. A stained glass window is over the front door.

Today the house belongs to the Valley Children's Hospital and is used as a thrift shop. It is ironic that the automobile which made this house possible will also probably lead to its destruction as it is in the path of a proposed freeway.

46

Russell C. Fey

The Porteous Home —
1095 North Van Ness Avenue

The stately home at 1095 North Van Ness was completed in 1911 at a cost of $8,000. The original owner, A.L. Munger, employed Hans Hansen who built many of Fresno's finer homes of this period.

The house represents a modified Greek Revival Style as the overall plan does not follow the normal rectangular box-type configuration. The second floor balcony is supported by large main Ionic columns rather than the smaller inset columns generally used to support such balconies.

It was in 1916 that James Porteous purchased the property and moved in with "a wife, six children, a German Shepherd, two cats and a bowl of goldfish." Mr. Porteous was born in Scotland in 1848. On the death of his father, he assumed the full responsibility for the care of his mother, brothers and sisters. Since he was the sole support of his family, he sought better opportunities by emigrating to California in 1873. He arrived in Fresno four years later. His first business was a blacksmith shop.

Having a knack for invention and a skill with machinery, he modified and improved an existing implement to create the famous Fresno scraper which was known and used around the world. He formed the Fresno Agricultural Works to manufacture the scraper on a large scale. He continued making inventions and the United States Patent Office lists over 200 patents registered in his name. They include ditch diggers, welders, the famous rotary harrow and even an airplane.

Agnes Porteous Walker, a daughter, remembers the curved driveway leading in from the street under the porte-cochere always lined with baby buggies, bicycles, scooters and wagons. The formal gardens were beautifully maintained by an English gardener. The rose garden was especially outstanding and greatly admired by townspeople.

After the death of Mr. Porteous in 1922, Mrs. Porteous sold the home. It was used as a rooming house, a rest home for the elderly, and is now the valley headquarters for the Boy Scouts of America.

The Miller Home — 1516 North Van Ness Avenue

Emma Miller and her husband, Dr. Walter Palmer Miller, both born and educated in Maine, came to the Valley in 1888, settling in the Sanger district where Dr. Miller practiced medicine and developed interests in the lumber business. It was here that Emma Miller started her forty-six years of reading activities by organizing a study club in Sanger. She was to become widely known throughout California as a "Shakespeare reader" and throughout the San Joaquin Valley as a book reviewer and lecturer.

In addition to her active career as a lecturer to clubs, Emma also was for twenty years a lecturer in English at Fresno State College. That her influence was wide can be shown by the founding of the Emma Miller Study Club in Fresno, named for her, and that she was highly honored can be evidenced by her trip abroad in 1925, financed by the Fresno Query Club as a token of esteem.

Courtesy Mrs. Ann Rue Hess

Well before World War I, the couple moved to Fresno and in 1917 acquired a two story frame farmhouse on North Van Ness and Home Avenues. With hipped roof broken by a dormer and with a deep porch across the front, the house is a familiar type frequently found in the Valley. The house first faced Home Avenue but had as its address 1506 North Van Ness. In the 1950's the Millers' daughter, Georgia, and her husband, Elief Rue, had the house turned around and moved to the lots next door. Structural changes were made and the house number changed to 1516 North Van Ness. A car wash establishment now occupies the former site.

Mrs. Miller died in Berkeley in April 1942. Dr. Miller, a graduate of Bowdoin College and a life member of the Fresno County Medical Society, predeceased her in 1927.

The Mosgrove Home — 660 East Pine Street

This two story frame bungalow at 660 East Pine Street, built in 1910 for Mr. and Mrs. William A. Mosgrove, was the first home to be constructed in this area north of Olive Avenue. Set in open land, the house gave Mrs. Mosgrove a good view of the mountains and when Mr. Mosgrove, an optometrist, went to San Francisco on the Santa Fe Railroad, he could see his wife waving from the front porch over half a mile away.

The house illustrates a comfortable and unpretentious style of living. The Mosgroves were newly married and Nellie Mosgrove's brother, Frank Faulkner, a Missouri architect, designed the house "just as Nellie planned it." The gable eave support indicates Stick Style and the chimney of river rock is a much used design element in the bungalows of this time. The living room fireplace is faced with local adobe tile. The house was built on a concrete foundation. Like homes in the Midwest, the house had a storm cellar reached by exterior doors that slanted upward toward the house. Above the cellar door was a "cookie window" with a wide shelf outside. This was for the three Mosgrove boys and their friends who gathered there on baking day. The sloping cellar door helped even the smallest child to reach the freshly baked cookies.

A veranda extending around two sides of the house and the wisteria covered arbor supported by columns provided old fashioned comfort but is not compatible in a stylistic sense with the rest of the house. In the only bathroom is a six foot long, claw footed bathtub.

The Main Home —
520 West
Princeton Street

This nine-room, red-brick house was constructed around 1914 by Mr. Eugene Main, who was the original owner. He had learned the trade of brick laying and brick making from his father and for several years after 1887 followed his trade, alternating between his home state of Missouri and Fresno. He settled permanently here in 1901 and thereafter actively contracted and built homes and public buildings.

Briefly he turned to brick manufacturing as stockholder and foreman of the Fresno Brick and Tile Works. When he built his own home he made all the bricks in his back yard, and when he finally sold the house he showed the next owners the only bad brick in the entire house.

Brick columns which support the porch are the most distinctive feature of the residence. Overall the house has a clean, uncluttered appearance. The

Russell C. Fey

texture of the brick contrasts with the wood of the eaves and frieze board.

At the time of the sale, 1945, there was nothing between this house and the old St. Agnes Hospital. Since then the land has been developed and new streets have been put in. The original address of 2805 North Fruit was changed to 520 West Princeton in 1948.

Russell C. Fey

Russell C. Fey

The Spencer Home — 395 North San Pablo Avenue

On the corner of North San Pablo Avenue and Klondike Street, a two story red brick house attracts the attention of the passerby. It was constructed by Wright H. Spencer about 1899 and features double brick walls with a six inch air space between for insulation and a screened porch surrounding the kitchen. An interesting feature is the "eyebrow" arrangement of bricks above the windows, a tedious job, as each brick must be carefully cut to create the curved arch. To reproduce such a design today would be very expensive.

Mr. Spencer was a relative of Platt Rogers Spencer, the originator of the Spencerian system of penmanship. His father, James, founded the city of Caro, Michigan and served as its mayor, deputy county treasurer and registrar of deeds as well as owning his own abstract office. Wright Spencer learned the abstract business working for his father and was well prepared to take his place in his new community.

He arrived in Fresno in April, 1888, during the great land boom when so many transactions took place every day that a veritable army of title searchers was required. He became a partner with Clark and McKenzie and they merged with three other abstract firms to form the Fresno County Abstract Company in 1891.

He resigned in 1918 to run for County Recorder, his motto being: "Thirty Years a Searcher of Records in Fresno County: honesty, efficiency, fidelity and courteous treatment." Always active in political affairs, he also served as superintendent of streets. His first wife, Josie Shields, daughter of a pioneer Fresno County family, died in 1907 and he married Alice Parrish of Los Angeles. At his funeral in 1928, honorary pall bearers were old friends from the Home Sweet Home Club, an organization well known in the 1890's. The family continued to occupy the home until 1937.

Photograph c. 1910.   Courtesy Mr. and Mrs. Charles Hiatt

Courtesty *Fresno Bee*

The Vincent Home — 921 North San Pablo Avenue

This fine Victorian house was the home of Mr. and Mrs. Joseph P. Vincent in the early 1900's. Many Eastlake influences are to be noted in this house of basically Stick Style design. The elaborate scroll work design in the pediment was made with lathe and handsaw. Spools and spindles decorate the porch which, when first constructed, wrapped around the south side of the house as well. An unusual feature is the double entry with one door into the "parlor" on the right and one leading directly from the front steps. The spindle-work bannisters on the stairs, newels and post railings are all band sawed. Made of clapboard siding one by fours, the house has fish-scale shingle design in the pediment.

The pioneer backgrounds of the Vincents were amazingly similar. Members of both families left Wisconsin heeding the call of the Gold Rush in 1849 and settling eventually in Sonora. The Vincents also lived for a time in San Francisco and then came to Stanislaus County. In 1865 the family of Elizabeth

Vivian Vincent also came to Stanislaus County.

Joseph P. attended San Francisco College which later merged with the University of California. He taught in Grass Valley and Nevada. During his term at a one-room school in Nevada he heard that the railroads were to meet in a week's time. He closed his school and was present at the driving of the Golden Spike.

Joining his family in Stanislaus County, he taught school and farmed. In 1870 he and Elizabeth were married. Twelve years later they moved to Fresno County, building a home on Temperance Avenue. Land prices were low here and he bought large acreages of raw land which were split in ten and twenty acre parcels, planted in orchards and vineyards, then resold. He was a promoter of the Enterprise Canal and Irrigation Company to bring water into the area.

Noting that children in the neighborhood had to go six miles to school, he circulated a petition to

continued on page 106

52

The Cardwell Home — 357 North Glenn Avenue

In spite of many changes through the years, this home is still a gracious reminder of Fresno's past. It was moved to this site from its original location near Broadway and Divisadero.

During its early years, the living room fireplace was the only source of heat in winter. When extensive remodeling and modernizing were done in 1945, the veranda was removed.

The William M. Cardwell family was associated with the house in its early days. Owned for a time by Frank and Nellie Short, it was deeded to his aunt, Melissa Wharton Cardwell, in 1911. Her husband, William, was a veteran of the Civil War, serving three years and eleven months with Company C of the 11th Missouri Cavalry. He came to Fresno in 1882 at the age of forty-five and started a contracting business. He also purchased vineyards in the West Park area and near Fowler.

He was active in the political life of Fresno, once being defeated in his bid for the office of Sheriff on the Populist ticket. The Cardwell's two sons were well known in Fresno. Bert was the stage manager of the old Hippodrome Theater and Frank W., a rancher near Sanger, was assistant postmaster for many years. Cardwell Station was named in his honor.

My Home In Fresno, a tapestry by Marguerite Thompson Zorach.

Photograph c. 1900.

Courtesy Mr. Tessim Zorach

The Thompson Home — 274 North Glenn Avenue

The home at 274 North Glenn was hardly unique when constructed early in the 1890's in the Altamont Addition north of Divisadero; one could not have guessed it would be preserved in a tapestry which hangs today in the National Collection of Fine Arts at the Smithsonian Institution in Washington, D.C.

Lawyer William Thompson brought his wife and two small daughters to Fresno in 1893. Late in the same year they purchased the Glenn Avenue house, and here Marguerite Thompson began to store the memories of a California childhood which she would one day record in wool and linen.

Marguerite graduated from Fresno High School in 1906, already certain of her future as attested by the yearbook: "best friend — paint brush, favorite resort — before easel; ultimately an artist."

Although enrolled at Stanford University in September 1908, she accepted an invitation from her aunt, Harriet Adelaide Harris, to join her in Paris.

On her return to California in April 1912, the young artist was described in a San Francisco newspaper article as a "Post Impressionist painter." The newspaper was quoted as feeling that her painting might be "a bit too modern to suit California temperament." Her family did not appreciate her style either and attempted to dissuade her from continuing as an artist by hiding her paints!

Fresno's genteel society was scarcely suited to her creativity and independence, and after a summer of camping in the Sierra, during which time she produced some dynamic paintings of the moun-

tains, Marguerite readied her first one-woman show for the Royal Galleries in Los Angeles. Included was *Plains of Provence*, a painting no longer exant, but described by one prophetic critic as a "velvety tapestry, so rich were the colors . . . "

The same show was held in Fresno at the Parlor Lecture Club in early December, 1912, after which Marguerite framed some of her most traditional works for her parents, saved some for herself, and then in her own words, "carted off amid protests all the old trash" — paintings, prints, drawings — to the city dump.

On December 24, 1912, Marguerite Thompson and William Zorach were married in New York. Fellow students in Paris, the two young Americans had associated themselves with the Post Impressionists there. They chose New York to live as the American city most accepting of modern art.

Both artists exhibited in the famous Armory Show of 1913, considered the watershed of early modern art development in the United States. William Zorach was to achieve considerable recognition as a sculptor, while Marguerite's creative energies for years were occupied with the production of the magnificent tapestries, which brought her fees of $1,000 to $20,000.

She described the tapestries and their creation: "I am first of all a painter. It was my interest in color (later in texture) and a certain spirit of adventure that led me to do a picture in wool . . . These works are built out of my life and the things that have

continued on page 106

The Hewitt Home — 175 North Diana Street

John C. Hewitt constructed this home in 1890 at 175 North Diana Street. A charming redwood frame Victorian with twin gables and a wide veranda on two sides, it features the fancy "gingerbread" and ornate spindles characteristic of its age.

Built five years before the arrival of the Santa Fe Railway on the corner of Diana and Alice streets (Alice was changed to Illinois in 1916) it was considered a fine residential neighborhood.

Mr. Hewitt was a native of Atlanta, Georgia and fought in the Mexican War. He came to California to engage in mining, but in 1852 turned to farming, his holdings consisting of 640 acres on Big Dry Creek.

In 1880 he married a widow, Mrs. Mary Morgan, mother of J.D. Morgan, a city marshall of Fresno. His son, Dr. John D. Morgan, remembers the house from his childhood days.

Shortly after his marriage, Mr. Hewitt sold his country property to invest very profitably in city real estate. According to his obituary in the *Fresno Weekly Expositor*, he was worth over $30,000 at the time of his death.

The present owner has lived in the house for fifty years and has divided it into apartments. It is very well maintained and today is still a most attractive house.

The McKay Home — 201 North Clark Street

Scott McKay, Deputy County Surveyor, built this house at 201 North Clark Street for his bride, the former Helen Jewett, shortly after their marriage in 1899. It has the elaborate shingle detail over the wrap-around porch popular at the time and in addition a two-room basement containing a living room and a kitchen, an adaptation beginning to take hold in Fresno in the early part of the century before air-conditioning had developed. About 1910 a sleeping porch was added, another popular Fresno feature designed to thwart the Valley heat.

Mr. McKay became County Surveyor and retained that position until his death in 1918 and members of the McKay family continued to occupy the home until 1944. Since that time new owners have added a large attic to the second story rooms, and it has become a rooming house.

Photograph c. 1910.

Courtesy Ayleen Wash.

The Rutherford Home — 230 North Clark Street

This elaborately decorated house at 230 North Clark Street was built in 1888 by James Rutherford, an experienced carpenter, for his wife and ten children one year after the family had moved to Fresno from Missouri. For Mr. Rutherford the trip was his second move to the West. Born in Kentucky in 1820 he had first moved to Missouri and worked as a carpenter. In 1850 he caught "California fever," crossed the plains by ox team and covered wagon and arrived in Hangtown (Placerville) where he panned for gold and worked in the building trade. The next year he returned to the East by way of the Isthmus of Panama and remained in Missouri for thirty-six years when once more he came to California attracted no doubt by the opportunities for carpenters in the booming 1880's.

For his new home he made an exceptionally interesting use of wood. The house follows basically the Stick Style. A fish scale divider course lies between the first and second stories providing a pleasing variation to the clapboard sides. Bay windows of the type so familiar in San Francisco are flanked by white painted pilasters which accentuate the vertical lines. A dentil course above the first bay contributes still another variation.

As a carpenter Mr. Rutherford also constructed the old Einstein School and helped build the old Hughes Hotel. In 1890 he moved to a ranch, and his first home in Fresno became the property of his daughters. The home has been in the family up to the present time and remains a source of pride. When one of his granddaughters, Ayleen Wash, built a new home recently she installed three stained glass windows taken from the old family home in her new residence.

The Hunt Home — 115 North U Street
(later The Bonsel Home)

Architect and builder of this home which is still occupied as a residence was Ben Hunt, an Indianan who came to California in 1885 and to Fresno in 1890. Mr. Hunt constructed his house in 1894 with a water tank in the loft since city water was not available to homes on the outskirts of town north of Divisadero.

As a result of later subdivision by the city, the house was moved north to fit on a lot and rotated one-quarter turn to face U Street. Widening of U Street and later installation of sewer mains have resulted in three different plantings of trees along the front of the property.

The house has hipped gables with a semi-classical pediment and with "returned cornices." The cornice line is not a full story above the porch line; therefore, the windows appear higher than in fact they are. Another feature of the house is the beautiful hand forged hardware on the doors. Some knobs are black porcelain with hand painted flowers.

Ben Hunt was one of the founders of the Valley Foundry and Machine Works in 1898. He sold the U Street home to C.R. Bonsel, an insurance agent, that year.

Mr. Bonsel was married to Annie Laurie Wishon, a member of the H.E. Wishon family. As the neighborhood became a favorite living area for influential Fresno families, the Bonsel's spacious home was used extensively for entertainment and neighborhood gatherings.

Although C.R. Bonsel died in 1921, one of his two daughters, Martha, continued to live in the house until 1973. According to Miss Bonsel, she introduced folk dancing to her classes in the schools.

The Berry Home — 306 North Second Street

This house is included, despite extensive changes from the date of construction about 1890, because it commemorates the memory of ebullient Fulton G. Berry. Berry was such a well known and popular hotel man and developer that the citizens gave his first name to one of Fresno's major streets. Born in Maine in 1834, he came to California in 1851 via the Isthmus of Panama and turned easily from gold miner to drayman, to groceryman, to realtor and finally to hotel proprietor. At one time he was a member of the San Francisco Stock Exchange. In financial straits, he moved to hustling Fresno in 1884 and recouped as manager and then as owner of the Grand Central Hotel on Mariposa Street near J (now Fulton). He was associated with every important business enterprise in the city. He owned city property and vineyards and was part owner of the electric light and gas utilities.

Located at 306 North Second Street, this one-story Victorian cottage with fish scale detail in the pediment, was owned but never lived in by Berry. It stands in the midst of Arlington Heights sub-division which he had developed with the touch of the born promoter.

Berry was a loveable prankster and his funeral, conducted according to his last wishes, continued the tradition. Held in the Elks Hall, a twenty piece band played *La Paloma, Home Sweet Home* and Mendelsson's *Spring Song* following which a funeral cortege moved through the town with the band playing airs. As the procession passed Grand Central Hotel which he had owned and operated for so many years, the band rendered *Auld Lang Syne*.

Russell C. Fey

60

Russell C. Fey

The Mundorff Home — 3753 East Balch Street

This one-story house at 3753 East Balch was designed and built by the brothers Charles and Henry Greene of Pasadena in 1917. Typical of Greene and Greene are the iron straps that fasten the drain pipes to the house exterior, basic U shape in design and exterior brick repeated in the interior fireplace. The Greenes built homes in which the interior and exterior were related through the use of materials. For example, beams supporting the wide overhangs outside are carried into the heart of the house. The house contains a sleeping porch at one end of the U and a separate butler's pantry, both features of Greene and Greene houses. Because the home on Balch is not completely typical of Greene and Greene southern California designs, it has been called Greene Colonial Style.

This is the only known Greene and Greene house in Fresno. The Greene brothers may be the least known of America's major architects, however, they have been described as the ones most expressive of their geographic and cultural setting. The Greene brothers worked in a unique mixture of Mission, Oriental and Swiss Chalet forms, emphasizing the horizontal and designing the lighting fixtures, carpets and furniture to complement the composition. A former owner of the Fresno home, not recognizing the distinctive shell motif of the wall lamps used by the Greene brothers, had them removed. The house was said to have been built as a wedding gift for Mrs. H.F. Mundorff and furnished from Gumps.

The Wishon Home — 3555 Huntington Boulevard

This spacious family home was built in 1915 by Albert Graves Wishon, pioneer of the electric power industry in the San Joaquin Valley. Located at 3555 Huntington Boulevard, the Wishon house with its truncated hip roof, bay windows, and portico extended by lattice work is a distinctive style. Such details are not usually used with stucco walls and tiled roof. Surrounded by a well groomed lawn, big trees and with the wide overhanging roof, it is reminiscent of a plantation house. Certainly the residence is similar to those of other well-to-do early twentieth century civic and business leaders in Fresno.

Besides the usual rooms found in family houses, this one contains a master bedroom suite, library, solarium, servants' quarters, and two sleeping porches. Due to Fresno's fierce summer heat, sleeping porches were considered almost a necessity before the days of swamp coolers and their successors, air conditioners. It is largely due to the vision and success of A.G. Wishon that Valley residents now have electric power to run the indoor climate modifiers which have made sleeping porches relics of the past.

Born November 6, 1858 at Coppeges Mill, Missouri, Wishon's early experience and interest in farming and civil engineering provided a foundation for his visionary development of irrigation systems which depended upon pumping plants powered by electricity from hydro-electric plants. Interested in electric power and convinced that the economic future of the San Joaquin Valley depended upon irrigation, Wishon built the Valley's first power plant on the Kaweah River east of Visalia, using capital secured through London connections. The Mt. Whitney Power Company commenced operations on June 30, 1899, after which Wishon used capital borrowed in San Francisco to finance installation of motors and transformers with Lindsay area pump irrigationists, thus beginning pump irrigation in the Valley.

Leaving the Mt. Whitney Company in 1902, Wishon became manager of the Fresno properties of the San Joaquin Electric Company, a firm bought out of receivership by Wm. G. Kerckhoff and A.C. Balch, Southern California hydro-electric power pioneers. The ensuing years saw competition for lighting business with the old gas company managed by Fulton G. Berry (for whom Fulton Street is named); competition for land to secure riparian rights to the north fork of the San Joaquin River; construction of an earthen dam at what is now Bass Lake to assure summer water flow, and expansion from an original capitalization of $500,000 to $150,000,000. Under Wishon's guidance the company extended operations into Kern, Tulare, Madera and Fresno counties and across the Coast Range to many coastal cities as well.

Although the company merged with Pacific Gas and Electric in 1930, A.G. Wishon remained a director and vice chairman of the board until his death in 1936. During these later years his interests expanded to include real estate, farming, manufacturing and finance. He was a stockholder in the ice manufacturing companies, a director for many years of Sun Maid Raisin Company, and with his son-in-law, Ralph W. Watson, operated extensive orchards and vineyards. The house is still occupied by members of the family.

This charming house at 1003 South Orange Avenue, in earlier days surrounded by a driveway and several acres of landscaped grounds, now has a frontage of eighty-seven and one-half feet. Eucalyptus trees provided cool shade and elms and date palms purchased from the old Roeding Nursery flourished.

The house which is built in the Stick Style has typical bracketed corners on the front bay at the cornice line and elaborately designed fish scale shingles in the gable. The porch, ornamented with spools and spindles, has decorative brackets attached to the hand-turned posts. A colored glass window catches the eye to the left of the front door and before time took its toll there was a somewhat similar colored pane in the bay window.

Mr. and Mrs. Raymond Robinson, who built the house, moved in on March 1, 1901 when the property was outside the city. At that time, Orange Avenue was at the edge of the city and the Hughes vineyard, across the street, was in the city. The property went into the city in the 1930's.

Robinson, who came to Fresno from Southern California in 1888 with Frank Romain, worked according to his daughter, for fifty-eight years for the same company, Griffen and Skelly, which later became the California Packing Company. Mrs. Robinson, who lived to be ninety-eight years old, came to Fresno in 1891. She remembered walking up the wooden sidewalk which ran from the Southern Pacific Depot to the Court House.

An elaborate stone wall and barbecue has been constructed on the rear of the lot by Mr. Herold Emmick, son-in-law of the Robinsons. Rock from the Kings and San Joaquin rivers has been arranged in the wall according to a systematic and repeated design. A sun-burst effect has been created by placing a large boulder in the center of each panel.

Russell C. Fey

The Robinson Home — 1003 South Orange Avenue

Russell C. Fey

Chapter Three

OUTLYING AREAS

When built many of these were farm homes. Today some are still rural, but most are in the metropolitan area.

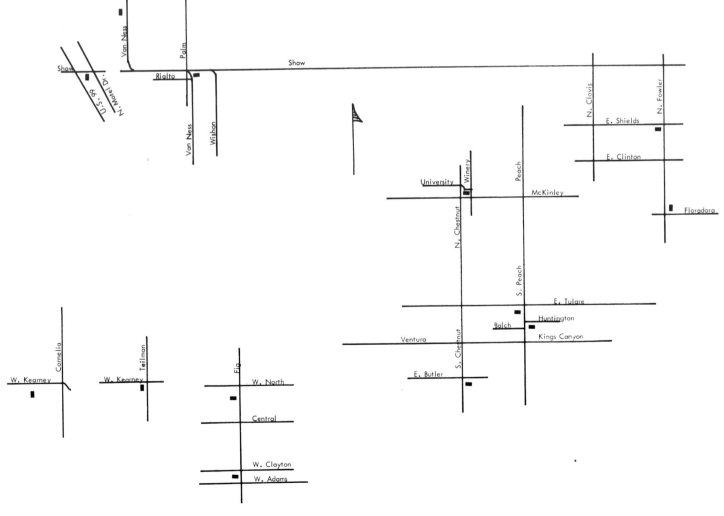

The Gregory Home —
4852 North Van Ness
Boulevard

Five miles north of downtown Fresno, in what is now a pleasantly wooded area known as "Old Fig Garden," J.C. Forkner and Wylie Giffen developed the Forkner-Giffen Tract of acre and half-acre residential lots. Cedar, deodar and other trees were planted along Van Ness Boulevard, and the developers brought electricity into the area, formed a water district, and persuaded the Traction Company and the Southern Pacific to extend the street car line north to the San Joaquin River. In 1919 they constructed five houses along the Boulevard. The house at 4852 North Van Ness is the only one of those remaining which stands virtually as it was built.

From the time it was built until 1941, this house was occupied by Fred W. Gregory, his wife and two sons. Mr. Gregory, sales manager for J.C. Forkner Fig Garden Incorporated, was credited with many land sales in the tract. It is said that folding tables and a tent were set up along the Boulevard from which Forkner and his salesmen conducted business.

Before 1919 Fred Gregory had been active in other ventures. In 1900 he operated Gregory and Company, a Mariposa Street store which sold bicycles, phonographs, and White sewing machines. In 1901, they added Oldsmobiles and Pierce Motorett automobiles, probably making Gregory and Co. Fresno's first automobile agency. Frank A. Homan, later Mayor of Fresno, joined the firm in 1903. The firm became Homan and Company in 1908, and did business in Fresno for many years under that name. During these years, Fred Gregory lived in San Francisco, operating a hardware store and selling a steam-propelled automobile called a White. Following the destruction of his store in the 1906 earthquake and fire, Gregory

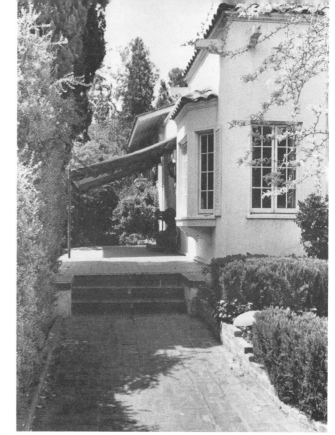

Russell C. Fey

returned to Fresno where he was associated with the fig packing business.

This stately home is a classic tri-level, built in a "U" shape around a courtyard and fountain. Distinctive features include a bay window and wainscoting in the dining room, a large master bedroom with arched windows and French doors opening onto a railed balcony, and a child's bedroom with windows on two sides which give the illusion of a tree house.

The bare earth which first surrounded this suburban house has long since vanished. Horace Cotton, a landscape architect, soon after graduating from the University of California, designed the plantings, and ordered the truckloads of trees and shrubs from San Francisco, which have given striking beauty to the grounds. The Gregory house facing south toward the center of town is reached by a driveway lined with twisted carob trees.

Photograph c. 1920.

66

Courtesy Mrs. L.L. Gregory

The Forestiere Home
5021 West Shaw Avenue

One of Fresno's most widely known dwellings is Forestiere's Underground Gardens, an underground complex of rooms, passageways and trees. The Gardens, lying under some seven acres of arid land in the northwest outskirts of Fresno, were created by Baldasare Forestiere, the second oldest son of a prosperous fruit grower in Messina, Sicily. In 1900, when he was twenty-one years old, Mr. Forestiere came to the United States where he worked at the underground construction of aqueducts and subways.

Courtesy Forestiere Underground Gardens

In 1903 or 1904 Forestiere came to Fresno, bought land where the Gardens are today, and prepared to plant an orchard. He discovered that trees would not flourish there because a thick layer of hardpan lay two feet or less below the surface. He also discovered that Fresno was very hot in summer. Remembering the cool subways in the East and recalling the coolness of caves and underground dwellings in Sicily, he began his own subterranean retreat.

First he dug a well some sixteen feet deep. It is now dry because the water level has dropped. Then he excavated his first house, planning construction so as to catch every breeze and to provide adequate ventilation and light. In each room he put a skylight which could be covered with glass in winter, stove with stovepipe reaching to the surface, and benches carved into the walls. Hardpan mixed with cement in a pleasantly random pattern was applied to the walls. Patches of concrete, remnants of each day's cement mix, cover the floors. The passageways are sloped so that rainwater will drain into sump pits.

Next Mr. Forestiere extended his excavations and dug out rooms where he grew citrus trees. He fashioned large round planters with skylights directly above and with the edges sloped so that rain would run into the planter. In an area twenty-two feet below the ground there are today several orange trees, one more than sixty years old and another one grafted with seven different kinds of citrus branches.

Everywhere there are arches, domed ceilings and windows with lovely views and pleasing vistas.

Eventually Mr. Forestiere constructed additional living quarters for himself which included a living room, kitchen, two bedrooms and a library. Today a small wood burning stove still sits, brightly blackened, and one may admire his ingenious plan to warm a bedroom by means of a stovepope from a fireplace that runs along the wall. The total complex includes a small, pleasant, dignified chapel.

As he grew older Mr. Forestiere dreamed of building and running an Italian restaurant within his unusual dwelling. He carved out an auto tunnel by which customers would enter, but he died in 1946 before he could complete the project.

How did Baldasare Forestiere build this remarkable complex? With a pick, shovel and a wheelbarrow to move the dirt. Later in life he used a Fresno scraper and a mule.

The Gardens are maintained by the Forestiere family and are open to visitors in good weather.

The Forkner Home — 6037 North Van Ness Boulevard

Northfield, the J.C. Forkner home at 6037 North Van Ness Boulevard was built in 1912, in a field seven miles northwest of Fresno on a boulevard 125 feet wide, newly planted with young trees and shrubs. Now beautiful eucalyptus trees and oleanders line the boulevard, and the ranch house, hidden by a giant carob tree and myriad other sheltering trees and vines, sits near the middle of the greatest fig producing area of the world, an area being rapidly transformed by the proliferation of spacious, suburban homes.

The house received its name because it was in the north field of the 12,000 acre Fig Garden District, an area divided by Bullard Avenue and located between Fresno and the San Joaquin River. Here Mr. Forkner successfully developed the largest single real estate development in the history of the county.

Designed by Swartz and Swartz, local architects originally from Kansas, the overall form of the house emanates from the early Prairie Style as indicated by the hipped, low profile roof. The dormers, however, are not traditional with this style. Large porches on the first floor and sleeping porches on the second floor gave an open, airy look to the residence. The house has a spacious kitchen, which in the Midwest might have been used to provide meals for the ranch "help." This was not the custom in California, but on many occasions it was used to help entertain prospective buyers of the Fig Garden lands. William Claybaugh, superintendent of Roeding Park, landscaped the grounds and planted the family orchard.

After living in the house for five years, the family moved to a home in the Forkner-Giffen tract, a newly-developed area of one-acre residential lots, now commonly referred to as the "Old Fig Garden," where they lived for some time before returning to Northfield.

During those years Northfield was occupied by the ranch foreman and his wife, and was made available to prospective buyers for Mr. Forkner's real estate projects. On one occasion forty-six potential customers sent here by Forkner's agents in San Francisco and Los Angeles were crowded into the house for the night.

"I had a superintendent whose wife was a good cook," recalled Mr. Forkner. "There is nothing like a homey atmosphere and well-cooked meals to create a receptive mood for a prospective customer."

1913 photograph courtesy of Mrs. J.C. Forkner.

Forkner, a graduate of the first class of the University of Kansas Law School in 1894, came west first to Los Angeles. His travels to the San Joaquin Valley, however, convinced him that Fresno was destined to be the Valley's largest city. After successfully developing land and settling immigrants in the Tulare Lake area, he came to Fresno in 1910.

Having learned from E.J. Wickson, a horticulturist at the University of California, George G. Roeding, a Fresno nurseryman, and Henry Markarian, a local farmer, that fig trees bore well in this area provided that their tap roots could reach the deep sandy soil lying from six inches to several feet under the hardpan, he acquired control of 12,000 acres of hardpan, hogwallow land located between Fresno and the San Joaquin River.

Twenty-five miles of irrigation canals and 135 miles of lateral ditches had to be built to bring water to the site. The land had to be levelled, first by six-horse teams drawing Fresno scrapers and later by forty-six of the first Fordson tractors, a Herculean task. Henry Ford, intrigued by the large purchase, made the trip to Fresno in a Model T to inspect the development.

Forkner's men used 660,000 pounds of dynamite to blast holes through the hardpan in order to plant 600,000 fig trees, the world's largest fig orchard. Additional holes were blasted for 60,000 ornamental trees and shrubs lining the eight-mile long boulevard extending from city limits to the river bluffs, and the eucalyptus, cedrus deodars and oleanders which line the avenues in the Forkner-Giffen tract (Old Fig Garden).

Old time residents tell of being taken out to the area as youngsters to watch the blasting. It was like an old-fashioned Fourth of July on a big scale. The newly planted fig trees, with their light green leaves looked like tomato plants, one woman remembered. Forkner estimated that it cost $600 to bring each acre into production. Most of the land was subsequently divided into twenty and forty acre plots for sale but the land nearest the city, the Forkner-Giffen Tract, was subdivided into one acre residential lots.

Mr. Forkner, noted for his belief in Fresno's future and a recognized authority on land settlement, spoke frequently to interested groups throughout the Valley and at the University of California. He died in 1969 at the age of ninety-six leaving his wife and four children. His widow, Lewella, whose parents were Mr. and Mrs. Lewis P. Swift, resides at Northfield.

The Teilman Home — 919 West Kearney Boulevard

Ingvart Teilman built this spacious stucco house at 919 West Kearney Boulevard in 1915. The general form and design features such as highly detailed cornices and low pitched, hip roof suggest the Italian Villa Style. Other features, the windows, the porch over the porte cochere and the balcony are a composite from many styles and have been added to assure comfortable living.

Mr. Teilman, for whom Teilman Avenue and the Teilman School are named, came to Fresno in 1878 from his native Denmark and for the next three years, did farm work including scraping in the Washington Colony and then took a job as carpenter in Madary's Planing Mill. Here his left hand was accidentally sheared off. Friends and fellow members of the Odd Fellows Lodge gave him financial assistance, and he went to San Francisco where he attended a business college and subsequently the Van Der Nailen School of Engineering. He returned to Fresno as a land surveyor.

Now his career followed closely the development of Fresno. He was a signer of the original petition to incorporate the city of Fresno in order to put in a sewer system. He subsequently helped to install it. In 1887, two years after incorporation, he became City Engineer. In the meantime he was active as a surveyor, laying out additions for the booming town and plats for the surrounding colonies. He acquired a ranch on Madison Avenue which his bride, the former Annie Kristine Holm, also a native of Denmark, helped to supervise. They were the parents of four children.

In these busy years he purchased a twenty-five acre strip from Van Ness to the Southern Pacific track for $25,000. He then divided the area into town lots and sold them for about double the purchase price. With the profits he purchased eighty acres on Kearney Boulevard on which many years later he was to construct the house discussed above. From 1896 until 1922 he was chief engineer for the Fresno Canal and Irrigation Company and actively associated with irrigation enterprises in the Laguna De Tache tract and elsewhere. He also designed the flume for the Sugar Pine Lumber Mill which carried timber into Madera. Most important of all his enterprises was helping to plan the Pine Flat project. In recognition of his services he was given the key which turned on the switch at the dedication of the great dam across the Kings River.

At the height of his career in 1915 he built his home on the eighty acre tract on Kearney Boulevard. It remained in the family until 1950.

KEARNEY MANSION

DOROTHY STUART

The Kearney Home — 7160 West Kearney Boulevard

The home of Martin Theodore Kearney, known today as Kearney Mansion, is one of four Fresno County sites listed in the National Register of Historic Places. Both architecturally and from the point of human interest, this building has a fascination all its own.

Martin Theodore Kearney (1842-1906) was a substantial contributor to the agricultural development of both Fresno County and the state of California. He began by managing a colony farming system for W.S. Chapman and Bernard Marks of San Francisco and devised a subdivision system whereby fencing and irrigation for all the lots in a colony were provided cooperatively. This enabled middle class purchasers to start farming without the tremendous financial outlay necessary had each been individually responsible for providing his own fencing and irrigation. Kearney advertised Fresno County far and wide, in the Eastern United States and in Europe, using various attractive promotional brochures which designated Fresno as a veritable Garden of Eden. Many settlers were drawn to the then arid but fertile county, and Mr. Kearney's prophecy turned out to be self-fulfilling, with credit to the labor of many settlers and farm workers, as Fresno grew from a dry desert to the richest agricultural county in the United States. Mr. Kearney, a raisin grower, was involved with the California Raisin Growers Association and worked toward better packing and marketing principles. Eventually the Sun Maid Raisin Company used many of Kearney's ideas.

By investing in and selling land on his own, Kearney increased his capital so that he could lay out the eleven-mile, three-lane Chateau Fresno Boulevard (now Kearney Boulevard) and the 240-acre Chateau Fresno Park, now known as Kearney Park. The boulevard was designed by Rudolph Ulrich, a well-known landscape architect from New York, who later designed for Chicago's Columbian Exposition, and it was planted with Australian eucalyptus trees, royal palms, flowering oleander, and

continued

71

pampas grass. Today, as ever, it is a beautiful scenic drive which evokes much praise. The park was open to the public in Kearney's lifetime. It was planted with many shrubs and trees; wild peacocks were imported to wander there freely and are still seen there today.

Mr. Kearney planned to build a magnificent French style chateau, but he did not live to carry out his dream. He had made several trips to Europe, and it is obvious that he was familiar with and a great admirer of Chateau de Chenonceaux in France. He dreamed of an even grander chateau in Fresno. Over the years he retained several architects (Willis Polk, Maurice Hebert and others) who designed various parts of an elaborate complex of buildings and gardens that were to surround magnificent Chateau Fresno. Only two buildings were completed before Mr. Kearney's death. The largest, intended to be the caretaker's lodge but known today as Kearney Mansion, became the residence of Mr. Kearney while he awaited completion of the grander chateau. The second and smaller building stands close by the mansion and was used for servants' quarters, kitchen, mess hall, and reading room. Today it houses a local history museum and gift shop.

The two buildings are excellent examples of French Renaissance architecture successfully simulated through the use of materials indigenous to this area, plus the use of Victorian stock classical moldings, all built by workmen employed by Mr. Kearney. Both buildings have a basic rectangular form with walls of two-foot-thick unstabilized adobe brick, covered with a thin coat of plaster on the exterior for waterproofing. The basic adobe structures are capped by a sophisticated roof structure, strongly influenced by the Schwab residence in New York City which itself was a copy of Chateau de Chenonceaux. The high roofs, dormer windows, ornate pinnacles at the intersection of the high roofs, the simple ridgemolding and lofty chimney stacks result in a picturesque skyline from a distance. With the effective horizontality of the Corinthian cornice superimposed on basic exterior walls of adobe brick, with all windows and main entrances enhanced with typical Victorian classical details, the total effect is that of a Franch Renaissance Chateau.

The interior of both units have typical Victorian classical details for trim, crown moldings, fireplaces and stair railings. In the main mansion, wall finishes are all imported wallpapers from France designed to Mr. Kearney's suggestions of very colorful, elaborate scenic representations. Decorative paper mache ceiling details in the main stair hall with appropriate period furniture in all rooms, combined with the colorful scenic wallpaper, yield an impression of a rich French Renaissance interior.

The foundations for the most magnificent part of the complex were being laid when Mr. Kearney set out on his last trip to Europe. He died on board ship, and the work on the Chateau ended with his life.

As it is, the Mansion stands as a historical landmark of architectural significance. At Kearney's death, his entire estate, amounting to $1,500,000 and 5,400 acres of some of the richest farm land of California, was left to the University of California. Kearney hoped that a college of agriculture would be established on his estate, with Kearney Park as the campus and the proposed Chateau Fresno as the administration building. However, the land was sold, with its revenues going to further agricultural research at the University of California, Davis, and other agricultural experiment stations. Thus again was Kearney a benefactor to the state's most important industry.

The park was not sold, however, but leased in 1949 to Fresno County, which has maintained it since. The mansion was used as a residence by the caretaker, Mr. Ralph Friselle, for a number of years. It was then vacant and fell into disrepair. A group of concerned citizens desired to preserve this important landmark, and went to work to save, restore, and to operate it as a museum for the public. The Fresno County Historical Society, to which the mansion was leased in 1962, continues to maintain and provide access to this fine home.

The Hansen Home — 3463 South Fig Avenue

The frame house at 3463 South Fig Avenue, the second oldest in this book, was built about 1877 by Jens Hansen who came to the San Joaquin Valley from Denmark. The house is said to be the first to be built in the Central California Colony, which was the first colony in the Fresno area.

Most early day farmers purchased land in twenty acre tracts from a land colony, an institution that today we would call a real estate development. Vast acreages had been secured initially by investors who used the land primarily for sheep grazing. Vineyards and orchards could not thrive until canals and irrigation ditches had been cut to bring water to the dry soil, a task requiring large scale financing and much time. Land colonies solved the problem. These colonies were not the usual cooperative bodies, but each proprietor owned his own tract, cultivating it as he chose as an individual farmer. A neighborly spirit of friendship and helpfulness prevailed.

Bernard Marks contracted in 1875 with William S. Chapman for twenty-one square miles of land in the Valley adjacent to Fresno. Six square miles in the center of the tract were subdivided into twenty acre farms, forming the Central California Colony. Twenty-three miles of avenues were laid out. The Fresno Canal and Irrigation Company's canal was extended to the tract. Vigorous advertising and other promotional work followed, and the "colonists," a sturdy and thrifty lot mostly from New England and the Scandinavian countries, began to come in.

The Hansen home was constructed mainly of one-inch by eight-inch redwood lumber hauled down from the Sequoias by horse and wagon. The one-story house originally had a front door opening nine feet high with a decorated glass panel above the door. Ceilings were twelve feet high to cope with the Valley heat. Large open porches on the north and south sides of the house have since been enclosed.

Soon after he arrived in California, Mr. Hansen, known to his friends as "Big Jens," sent to Denmark for the nineteen year old young woman who became his bride. Upon arriving in Fresno, she went immediately to Kohler's boardinghouse. The story goes that she could not communicate with anyone, but silently waited for her prospective bridegroom. When he drove up with horse and wagon, she flew to the window crying the only English she knew, "My man! My man!"

Hansen, who began farming with forty acres, later increased his farm to 120 acres. He raised peaches, nectarines, quinces and pears which were dried and sold to the local packing houses. At one time he sold fresh figs to the New York market. About twelve years ago the family put about sixty acres into prunes, which they raise in addition to cotton and grapes.

A member of the fourth generation of the family now has an interest in the ranch and will continue to produce crops in the tradition of this family of thrifty farmers.

Photograph, 1887.

The Rowell Home — 6635 South Fig Avenue

The name Rowell has been well known in the Fresno area for one hundred years. William Franklin Rowell was the third Rowell brother to migrate to California. Dr. Chester Rowell, one of Fresno's first physicians arrived here in 1874 having come to the Pacific Coast in 1866. He was to carry on a wide practice, be three times elected a State Senator, become Mayor of Fresno, a regent of the University of California and founder of a newspaper, the *Fresno Republican*. Next came Albert Rowell who migrated in 1873, settling in the Selma area. William Franklin Rowell arrived in 1883.

He was born in Woodsville, New Hampshire, the son of Jonathan and Cynthia Abbott Rowell who moved west in 1849 with their eight sons and settled near Bloomington, Illinois. The father died only a year after the move and the young sons worked hard to support the family. W.F. and four brothers served in the Union Army during the Civil War.

In 1883, after looking over the region, W.F. bought property in Washington Irrigated Colony, usually known as Washington Colony, and one of the most notable of the many colonies of small farmers.

In the following year, 1884, Mr. Rowell built this nine room redwood home, at 6635 South Fig Avenue, on his new acreage near the village of Easton. The old farmhouse is of simple style with none of the ornamentation and detail that became so common in the 1890's. The floor plan is a rectangle with the conventional veranda on two sides of the structure. The redwood lumber used for construction had to be hauled down from the mountains by wagon.

In addition to developing various ranch properties, Mr. Rowell was active in the first cooperative raisin association and had a cooperative packing house at Easton. Recognized as a community leader, he was elected representative to the State Legislature from the sixty second district. While serving as legislator, he introduced at his friend John Muir's request, the bill which made Yosemite a state park.

On retirement, he sold the ranch to Godfrey Jacobsen who was working for him. Godfrey's son Milo, who was born in the house, occupies the property at present. So for over ninety years, the family house has been lived in by only two families.

When he retired, W.F. moved to San Jose where he died on April 13, 1912, predeceasing his brother, Dr. Chester, by just ten days. He was survived by his widow and six children. His son, Milo L. Rowell, was well known as a promoter of the Sun Maid Raisin Association and owner and manager of downtown Fresno business property.

74

The Steinwand Home — 228 South Peach Avenue

This shingle covered home at 228 South Peach Avenue was designed and built about 1898 by the first owner, Joseph Steinwand, an experienced carpenter. Mr. Steinwand, as a boy, had been sent to America from Germany by his father to escape conscription in the German army. After living in Chicago and Oakland, he and his wife, also a native of Germany, purchased twenty acres near Fresno where they raised figs, olives and grapes. In addition, Mr. Steinwand worked as a carpenter, and his hand made tools are now prized possessions of his grandson.

Set on a brick foundation, some of the distinctive features of this ranch house are a full basement, arches on the porch and an octagonal tower on the east side. The line of the hip roof is broken by two dormers. The entire exterior is shingled.

The interior was equally distinctive and possessed a strong Teutonic flavor. When first constructed, the entrance was through a front door flanked by glass side panels and topped by an ornate fan glass into a vestibule. Beyond stretched a "great hall," tall and narrow, from which hung two large pink, hand painted, kerosene chandeliers. A large table was in the center of the room. At the far end were china cabinets holding Bavarian pieces. Off the hall and in the octagonal tower was a small parlor, complete with rocker, foot stool and needlepoint Victorian chairs. A grandchild remembers the room as having "an air of Sundays only."

Other buildings included a big barn, a carriage house and a building for brine barrels where olives were cured. Still another building was used to bottle and label wine produced on this early day Fresno ranch. A water tower, "cool and dank," still stands.

Four Steinwand children were raised in the Peach Avenue home. Albert became a dentist and Oscar a physician, both practicing in the Sanger area. Otto was an inventor, working for S and W Foods, perfecting machinery and products. Harriet, a biology teacher, naturalist and friend of John Muir, became the first woman lookout in Tahoe National Forest at the turn of the century. It was said that she "could shoe a mule and pack a horse and yet serve tea with grace." The Steinwand boys were musicians and active in the development of the Fresno Symphony League.

Russell C. Fey

Russell C. Fey

The Euless Home — 373 South Peach Avenue

The modest but lovely country home of John Euless, constructed by E.J. Farr in 1913, now stands on one and one-half acres of beautifully landscaped grounds at 373 South Peach Avenue at the corner of Huntington Boulevard. The most distinctive feature is the hooded dormer. The upstairs sleeping porch, broad eaves, deep porch and cement basement are all common features of Valley homes and were to "beat the heat."

Mr. Euless came to Fresno in 1906 from Tennessee and engaged in the real estate and insurance business. In the 1930's he helped to develop an oil enterprise in the Coalinga district and was a member of the committee that represented grape growers-at-large in Washington, D.C. in negotiations concerning government purchase of Muscat, Thompson and Sultana Grapes. Active in community affairs, he was also interested in sports and led a subscription drive to construct the baseball park appropriately named John Euless Baseball Park. He loyally supported the Fresno State College teams and for several years awarded a $100 scholarship to an unusually proficient player, preferably a pitcher. He is said to have been primarily responsible for bringing professional baseball to Fresno and was a liason man for the St. Louis Cardinals.

Showing an unusual combination of architectural styles, this substantial home at 4881 East University, which faces Winery Avenue, was built in 1914 for Fred M. Roessler. Hans Hansen, the builder, was a popular local contractor responsible for many similar homes in the area.

The major feature is the front portico in the Greek Revival Style, composed of three (an unusual number) Ionic columns two stories high, and supporting on the hipped roof a hipped roof dormer. A second floor balcony is surrounded with a decorative balustrade. The main door is off center: a semi-elliptical opening with a flat plain door frame flanked by two side panels of beveled, leaded glass and topped by a glass fan light. The porch is a straight open veranda on a base of cement. The symmetrically placed second floor windows have a flat double sash. A grape arbor leads to the north entrance.

Across Winery Avenue stands the tank house and winery building, now used as a part of the Fresno Museum of Natural History.

Fred M. Roessler, born in 1857 in St. Martin, Reinish, Germany, was the son of a viticulturist. At sixteen, he left home to see the world. Coming to America, he enlisted in a nautical school and sailed the Pacific to the Far East.

An article about California grapes encouraged him to come to Monterey where he worked as a farm hand. Looking for an area to locate, he came to Fresno because of the low land costs. His first holdings of forty acres were purchased for $1600. He improved this vineyard and gradually added land until he owned 180 acres. Roessler began producing wine commercially in 1892 and constructed his large building a year later.

Roessler was married to Sina Johnson in 1890. They had three children, a daughter and two sons. In addition, they adopted a son.

The home, now used as the administration building of the California Christian College, still retains the ornamental and shade trees that made it a show place of the district.

The Roessler Home — 4881 East University Avenue

Russell C. Fey

77

The Giffen Home — 4824 East Butler Avenue

Wylie Giffen, a farmer with extensive holdings in Fresno County, built this beautiful Tudor Style home in 1916. Mr. Giffen's operations covered a wide variety of crops but he is probably best known for his grapes and raisins. At one time, his 1,320 acre property was the largest Muscat vineyard in the world, and his Thompson vineyard was the world's largest in 1912. His vast Lucerne and American Vineyards were showplaces of the San Joaquin Valley. He was one of the founders of the California Associated Raisin Company and for many years was the president and manager of the Sun Maid Raisin Growers Association. In later years, he added several thousand acres of wheat and cotton to his farming operation.

Russell Giffen, one of Wylie's two sons, continued to add to the family's holdings until 1946, when he sold all his interests to Anderson Clayton and Company, as reported in *The Fresno Bee*, for $7,000,000. Rated the largest individual farmer in the world, Russell eventually extended his operation to over 55,000 acres on the West Side where cotton, flax, wheat, barley and vegetables were raised.

Wylie Giffen built the spacious home for his wife and three children and the family lived there and farmed the surrounding land until 1923, when the land was subdivided. The English Tudor Style is reflected in the high gabled tile roof with no eaves, inside brick chimneys, and exterior stretcher bond brick on the lower level, with wood trimmed stucco on the upper level. The upstairs rooms open into a large central hall with a stained glass skylight, through which prisms of colored light reflect on the walls and floor.

Now owned by Pacific College, the house is used as the administration building for the Mennonite Brethren Biblical College Seminary. Although there have been minor alterations to accommodate current needs, none of the walls, woodwork or trim have been changed.

78

Russell C. Fey

The Hines Home — 2893 North Fowler Avenue

John Newton Hines and his family were prominent in the early development of Fresno. Born and raised in Tennessee, he was graduated from college in 1884 and came west to Fresno where he began work as a bookkeeper for Kutner, Goldstein and Company. Because of poor health, he was ordered to give up his indoor work.

He and his brother bought teams of horses and hauled lumber from Pine Ridge. His health regained, Mr. Hines sold his teams, and with John Albin as a partner, then ran the old Pleasanton Hotel. He and his two brothers then started a prosperous grocery business on the corner of I (Broadway) and Fresno. In 1916, he sold his interests in the business to devote more time to his vineyards, farms and real estate holdings.

Mr. Hines' marriage to Annie May Owens is of special interest. She is said to have been the first baby girl born in Fresno. Mrs. Hines lived her entire life in Fresno where she and Mr. Hines raised six children.

When Mr. Hines built this two story, rectangular home for his family at 2893 North Fowler Avenue he departed from the conventional type of house for the Valley. Considered an expensive home, it is one of the few brick homes shown in this book and is distinguished from all others by the open joint at the outside corner and darker brick used for ornamentation in the bays, windows, porch pillars. It features stretcher bond red brick with header bond at the second story level. The narrow, arched windows with "eyebrow" detail set into the wall add light and charm to this spacious house. The entry is recessed and supported by one brick pillar.

The Forthcamp Home — 6158 East Floradora Avenue

The Forthcamp home at 6158 East Floradora basks in a tranquil setting of clipped hedges, junipers and stately old trees that join harmoniously with the surrounding vineyards. Constructed in 1913 by John Jasper for Mr. Ernest August Forthcamp and his mother, the family has continually occupied the home since that time. In Western Stick Style, as the gable brackets prove, the boulders in the foundation and chimney are an unusual feature for this style. However unusual, they provide an attractive variation to the predominantly wood construction.

First member of the family to arrive in Fresno was John D. Forthcamp who emigrated from Germany to America as a young man. Two years later he arrived in California and began a stock business that was to give him recognition as a pioneer sheep man of the San Joaquin Valley. In 1874 he came to Fresno County, ranging his flocks on the broad expanse of plain and desert where the city of Fresno now stands. As Fresno grew, John Forthcamp platted sixty acres into residential tracts, cut a street through the center and named it Forthcamp Avenue (now North Fulton). He then purchased twenty acres of land in what was then Temperance Colony, where he established a new home. Here he set out a small vineyard, one of the first in the Valley.

His first wife was a daughter of Moses Church, and they were the parents of a daughter. After the death of his wife he married Lena Pannemann, and their son, Ernest August was born August 19, 1884. Two years later the elder Forthcamp died, but Lena and her second husband, Mr. Fred Ehlert, continued to operate the place.

The son, Ernest Forthcamp, attended Fresno High School and the Chestnutwood Business College of Fresno. At age eighteen, he began managing and operating the Forthcamp property, resetting and planting new vines. As he prospered, he added land until there were 140 acres in the Forthcamp Vineyard, served by its own packing plant. In these years of expansion he and his mother built the home. Ernest Forthcamp lived with his mother and remained a bachelor until 1942 when he married Henny Pannemann. Mr. Forthcamp died in 1957.

Chapter Four

OTHER COMMUNITIES

These communities developed with the coming of the railroad, with the exception of Centerville, Fresno County's oldest existing settlement, which was a station on the Stockton to Los Angeles stagecoach line.

CENTERVILLE
CLOVIS
DEL REY
FOWLER
KINGSBURG
REEDLEY
SANGER
SELMA

Centerville

First comers to the vicinity of Centerville established a small settlement at the stage road crossing of the Kings River named Scottsburg, after W.Y. (Monte) Scott who ran a saloon and eating place there. When the citizens flooded out in the winter of 1861-62 and again in 1867, they moved to higher ground and changed the name of the trading center to Centerville.

Here a flour mill, a two story hotel, a blacksmith and wagonmaking shop, stores, saloons, a post office and, for a time, the only church in the county made Centerville the rival of Millerton and Fresno. Centerville received serious consideration for the county seat in 1874 when Fresno was chosen, and by 1882 the town had 800 residents and three physicians to take care of them.

Cattle-raising was big business then, as now, and one of the first and biggest cattle raisers was William (Yank) Hazelton, who came to California in 1849 and to the San Joaquin Valley in 1853. He founded what is still known as the Hazelton Ranch where the Kings River comes out of the foothills. Succeeding generations of Hazeltons have continued to operate the ranch. Hazelton's wife, Mary Jane, was an Akers, a member of another early Kings River family. She is said to have planted the first orange tree in the San Joaquin Valley.

A few citizens who were children in Centerville during its heyday remember it as a quiet, non-roistering town, a pleasant place in which to live. The I.O.O.F. hall was available for entertainment and dancing to the strains of the fiddle.

There were green trees and lots of water. The housewives were relieved of their weekly washing chore by Indians who would build a fire in the yard to heat kettles of water for their work.

Two one-time Negro slaves, Mr. and Mrs. Gabriel Moore, are credited with planting the first apple and fig orchard near Centerville.

Eric Mitchell

The Caldwell Home —

19 North Oliver

Centerville

The *Fresno Weekly Expositor* published at Millerton, November 15, 1871, states that "Mr. Caldwell of Centerville proposes building a brick house 22' x 36' adjoining his hotel, to be occupied as a private dwelling by himself and family." The hotel, a two-story wooden structure which was on the Stockton to Visalia stage line, burned before 1900, but the house stands today at 19 North Oliver, one of the oldest houses in Fresno County and the oldest to be shown in this book.

In sharp contrast to many of the earliest homes that were hastily constructed this house was built to last. Constructed of bricks made locally, by the Woods brothers according to local tradition, the walls are of solid brick, three tiers thick. Except for slight deterioration of mortar in spots the house remains after 104 years as originally constructed except for the floors which have been replaced and a porch which was added sometime later — date uncertain.

Entrance doors and windows have been set in wooden frames within the walls, which are about fourteen inches thick. A lime plaster has been applied to the interior walls and to the ceiling, eleven feet high where heavy hand-made laths provide the base for the plaster. As might be expected, the house is cool in summer and warm in winter. Surrounded today by trees and vines the house appears to be a serene part of the quiet countryside.

Russell C. Fey

83

Clovis

Clovis, named for Clovis M. Cole, a prominent early day grain rancher, arose in 1892 around a railroad station constructed twelve and one-half miles from Fresno on the San Joaquin Valley Railroad, a line designed to bring timber from the Sierras to a newly constructed lumber mill at the station. Today the lumber mill is gone and Clovis, a town of approximately 20,750 inhabitants, has modern stores, repair shops and service industries. It lies immediately adjacent to the city of Fresno. Once a year the Clovis Rodeo, reminder of the days of the great Valley ranches, draws large audiences to see nationally recognized performers.

The Hays Home — 4735 North Temperance

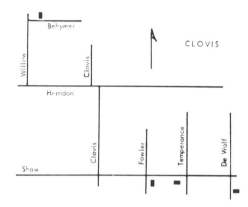

This simple frame house retains the flavor of the early pioneer homes of this area. It is basically rectangular with a number of projections. The use of wood for both structure and trim is well exemplified. The front pedimented gable and porch are decorated with attractive Eastlake style spindles. The main entrance at the center of the house is one of its most pleasing features — open cement steps, wood porch flooring, three turned post supports, open veranda and balustrade of turned posts. An oak door has glass in the upper portion and is topped by a glass transom. A large screened porch on the back of the house connects with the plain tank house.

The house was constructed in 1903 by Nathan Henry Hays, who came to California from Wisconsin with his wife, Emily Cork in 1899. They lived in the Easton area until the ranch in Clovis was developed. Ressie Reyburn, a daughter, remembers

seeing her mother drawing house plans on a cracker box. The nine children were raised in this home in which education was considered a "must" and most attended college.

The ranch was planted to peaches and grapes. Industrious farmers, the family still found time to be active church members. An incident which occurred one Sunday was a severe shock. During the church services their buggy and team of horses disappeared and were never found. This was indeed a severe loss since Mr. Hays traveled often on business and replacement was quite costly.

Russell C. Fey

84

The Reyburn Home —
4538 North DeWolf
Clovis

Joe Reyburn left Iowa in 1862 and joining a wagon company travelling with mule teams came to Oregon. After one year in the rainy Willamette Valley he moved south, first to Nevada and eventually to California in Salida, Stanislaus County. Here he married Mary Ella Lester who was from Iowa, homesteaded 320 acres of land and raised grain. In 1881, amidst a land boom, he sold his Salida property and purchased four sections of land from the German Syndicate east of Clovis. He and his family lived in this small house until 1891, then moved to a very large home on Barstow Avenue, which has since been torn down. Mr. Reyburn remarried and had six children by his second wife. The family was very active in the community, well thought of, and as one daughter-in-law put it, they "had a way" with people.

Russell C. Fey

The house at 4538 North DeWolf, built in 1881, is of a style that can best be described as an honest and straightforward example of "shelter" as built by early settlers in this area. It is a type of building which is fast disappearing but was not uncommon a number of years ago. No effort has been made to ornament — all is utilitarian and inexpensive. It is of board and batten construction, but differs from present day construction in that the large vertical boards act as the load carrying members of the walls, in addition to being the weather shield. There are no stud walls with finish applied inside and outside. The battens are nailed over the boards and the joints between the boards to provide a weather seal. The boards and battens are of redwood, which had been locally available. Redwood (along with cedar) is the only wood that would stay in one piece for a long period of time when stuck so deeply into the ground. A chemical property of this wood makes it decay resistant and relatively secure against termites. The windows are handled straightforwardly; a hole cut out in the wall and the window nailed on.

The original house was small; a living room, lean-to kitchen, two bedrooms and porch were added later. A large kitchen was added in the late 1880's. These additions were carried out in the same motif as the original house, and the building looks as one.

A fig tree stands in the front yard and is said to be over eighty years old.

Russell C. Fey

The Sharer Home — 6177 East Shaw Clovis

This delightfully well-maintained house, which can be classified as a Stick Style building with the Eastlake decorative elements, is finely proportioned and shows an obvious concern with beauty and style. A fine example of Victorian architecture of the 1890's, the house illustrates the many and fascinating possibilities to be found in the use of wood by builders of that day. Of wood frame construction, with wood shiplap siding applied horizontally, it has fish scale shingles on all the gable ends. These gables are decorated with spindle work, as is the entire length of the front, open veranda. Stained glass in the front door and transom panels in the bay windows add a lovely touch of·color. A tank house at the rear of the house has simpler but similar detailing. The cupola on the barn was built by Clovis Cole.

John William Sharer came to Fresno County from Illinois in the boom year of 1887. After living and working around the Enterprise area for several years, he married Nellie Dawson, a neighbor girl. He purchased the property at 6177 East Shaw Avenue in 1890. The present home there was begun in 1892, and it was added onto until well into the 1900's. Most of the lumber for the house was hauled by Mr. Sharer from the old Peterson Mill in the mountains beyond Toll House. He found it profitable in the fall of the year to haul lumber from the mountains for the building of many of the homes in and around Clovis. "He hauled lumber down the old, old Toll House Road," recalls one of the three children.

Mr. Sharer was an enterprising and progressive viticulturist and an authority on the laying out of fine vineyards. During the years 1890-94, he and his brother set out the first piece of vineyard in the Enterprise Colony. He was one of the original organizers and officers of the Melvin Grape Growers Association (which became a member of the California Fruit Exchange.) An astute businessman involved in many business affairs, he still found time to devote to service in his church. His wife and three children shared this home and his interest in his various business enterprises and his church.

The Browne House —
3354 Behymer
Clovis

J.W. Browne, Sr. paid twelve dollars and fifty cents an acre for the half section of land on Behymer Road northwest of Clovis in 1884. Mr. and Mrs. Browne, with their five children, came from Missouri, living a short time in Modesto before coming to the Clovis area. They were encouraged to locate here by a brother-in-law who raised race horses.

J.W. Browne, Jr. was born in a small house on the ranch in 1884. With a growing family of seven children, the Brownes planned a larger dwelling. In 1890 sugar pine logs for the future house were cut at Ockenden near Shaver Lake and hauled by team to the farm where they were seasoned for a year. They were then taken to the Madera Planing Mill and processed into lumber. The lumber used in building was carefully selected so that there were no knotholes exposed in any part of the original house.

Russell C. Fey

In 1916 J.W. Browne, Jr. and his wife Mary, purchased the property, paying $125 an acre. Originally the house had five bedrooms, a dining room, parlor, kitchen and bath. Between the dining room and the stairway to the bedrooms upstairs there was an open breezeway. On cold and windy nights the lamps often blew out.

The dining room was paneled alternately with pine and redwood. All the rooms were large with twelve foot ceilings. Dark wood was used for the stairway railing and the front door was elaborately carved. The younger Brownes modernized the house and put in a foundation. The cost of the cement and redwood foundation was sixty dollars. Plumbing was added to the kitchen, porches were enclosed and enlarged, partitions were removed, one porch became a sun room and the breezeway was enclosed.

Mr. Browne, Jr. lived on the farm for seventy-two years when poor health necessitated moving. Mrs. Mary Browne recalls many parties and family gatherings, including the fiftieth wedding celebration of the senior Brownes.

Although modernized several times, the house retains most of its original charm. The gables are decorated with shingles in a fish-scale design, and the porch is supported by turned posts topped with fancy wooded ornamentation.

The present owners have furnished the home with antique pieces representative of the period in which the house was built. The garden still contains many of the original trees and shrubs.

Del Rey

Del Rey, a town of about 900 people, is located on what was formerly part of the Del Rio Reyes (River of the Kings) ranch. First settlers on the site were the A.T. and J.R. Wilkinson families from Ohio, who purchased eighty acres of land for $12.50 per acre in 1884. Today similar land in this area when leveled and converted into vineyards would sell for about $3,000 per acre. From this little town, dried fruit packing houses send their products throughout the world.

The Welsh Home — 9486 East Lincoln   Del Rey

Among the elegant homes in the Del Rey area is one called the "Crown Jewel" of McCall Avenue. Its actual location is at 9486 E. Lincoln Avenue. A visible symbol of the wealth and grand style of living that came into the Valley as the oil and viticulture industries flourished, it is a harmonious adaptation of the "Prairie" or northern colonial style so much in vogue in the early 1900's.

This beautiful home was built by Harry W. Welsh, a pioneer valley oilman, rancher and lawyer. He hired architect Joseph Blick of Pasadena, to design and supervise the building. Because of the tremendous task of assembling materials, it took two years to build this colonial mansion. Construction began in 1912. Though Mr. Welsh died in 1945 and the house passed to other owners, the house is pretty much as he left it. The original furnishings, paint and wallpaper remain.

As balanced and symmetrical as the exterior is, with its matching pillars, windows and dormers, it is the interior which makes the house unique. The interior is Spanish cedar, enameled white. The wood trim is mahogany and the wallpaper is mulberry and gold — "hangings" as Mrs. Welsh called it. Solid brass fittings throughout, cut glass doorknobs, and one entire wall of the library of cut, leaded glass, provide luxurious surroundings for the owners of this four-story, twenty-eight room mansion.

Courtesy *Fresno Bee*

88

When Thomas Fowler, a boisterous, likeable and energetic young Irish immigrant, first saw the San Joaquin Valley in the 1850's, he could not have guessed that a town would be named for him and that the unfenced grazing land for sheep and cattle would be transformed into green vineyards and citrus groves. Fowler, one of many towns that sprang up in the 1870's along the route of the Central Pacific Railroad, began when Fowler, then a State Senator and the owner of thousands of cattle, started to ship his livestock from a railroad siding (Fowler's Switch) in 1872. Ten years later a few pioneer families had gathered near the site and the characteristic scramble for real estate had begun. A town was platted in 1882, and although Fowler never lived within fifteen miles of the town, the residents adopted his name for the community.

A Southern Pacific railroad depot was put up, followed by houses, schools, and churches. Settlers rushed in to the surrounding area to raise wheat, barley and oats by the dry farming method. Gradually the stark landscape softened as trees and shrubs matured. Water from irrigation ditches reached the fields. Orchards and vineyards appeared. One woman remembered from these early days that the gasoline engines first used to pump water made Fowler's fields very noisy. A peaceful, rural town, Fowler was incorporated in 1908.

Fowler

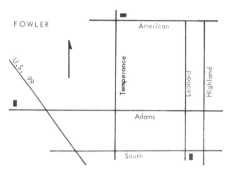

The Judge Nye Home
4818 E. Adams
Fowler

Stephen Girard Nye was born in Westfield, New York in 1834, of "Puritan stock" according to family records. He began teaching school at the age of 16 to finance continued study toward a law degree. Coming to California in 1861, he taught in Alameda County until being admitted to the bar. Subsequently he served as District Attorney of San Leandro and as a judge of the Superior Court from 1869 until 1875. He also was elected State Senator in 1880.

He had married a former student from his New York teaching days, Miss Emma Hall, and during their years in Alameda County they acquired ranch property in the Woodlake and Fowler areas. Following his term in the Senate, he retired to the Woodlake ranch and planted the first orange groves in the area. After resuming his law practice from 1890 to 1904, Judge Nye again retired and this time

Courtesy Emma Welch

they moved to the 200-acre Fowler ranch and constructed a large home. He called it "Emma Vineyards" after his wife and raised figs and peaches in addition to grapes. The big house was situated on a rise and was painted barn red with white pillars. But Judge Nye was to enjoy his new home only two years before his death from a stroke in 1906.

89

The Young Home
4822 S. Temperance, Fowler

Isaac Young, born in Sumpter County, South Carolina on April 17, 1855, came to California in 1888. An outstanding Black pioneer of the area, a teacher, farmer and local minister, he received his education through the United Presbyterian Church. He owned property in Fowler at a time when there were approximately forty Black families in the area, and then in 1904 he purchased the twenty-acre ranch at 4822 South Temperance, three miles east of Fowler, from O.J. Woodward. The land was not irrigated but a stream ran across one corner, and from this stream the family carried water for the trees and vines until irrigation water was available. Mr. Young raised grapes, peanuts, watermelons, peaches, alfalfa, vegetables and a little tobacco. He

Courtesy Eric Mitchell

lived in the frame house with his family, adding the second floor in 1916.

On May 9, 1904 he married Mary D. Garlington, and to this marriage eight children were born. Rhoda, his first wife, had borne him six children. Mr. Young gave his time generously to his local church, conducting programs and holding picnics on his ranch on special occasions. A humanitarian, he helped many people journey to Fowler. Mr. Young died June 8, 1948 at the age of 93 years.

The Jamieson Home — 9801 East South Avenue, Fowler
(later The Smith Home)

Russell C. Fey

The tradition is that Mr. James Jamieson purchased several sections of raw land east of Fowler and five miles north of Selma during the early 1880's. The home, tank house, barns and corrals were built about 1883. Eventually Mr. Jamieson subdivided much of the acreage, which local deeds list as being in the Jamieson Colony.

The large barn and corrals, the eucalyptus grove and pastures that were still in use in 1902, when

Alfred J. Smith purchased 240 acres, indicate that Mr. Jamieson dry farmed his land in grain.

The house was built on a popular early plan with a central core of rooms: a kitchen fourteen by eighteen feet and a "sitting room" fourteen by sixteen feet, with porches all around the house for protection from the heat of summer and the driving rains of winter.

The main floor of the house was five feet above ground level, and a five-foot excavation had been dug under the kitchen and "sitting room," making a spacious and cool basement, where fruits and vegetables could be stored.

The outside walls are made of uprights of one-by-twelves covered with clapboards and lined with tongue-and-groove for walls and ceiling alike. The foundation timbers are redwood twelve-by-twelves. The double-hung windows are six feet tall with six panes in each half. Pegs with springs hold them in position.

The porches on two sides are covered by shingle roofs so that a screened utility porch on the south entrance could provide a sink with cold running water, a roller towel rack and pegs and deer horns to hold the men's hats and outdoor coats. On the

continued on page 106

90

Kingsburg

The story of Kingsburg illustrates the history of the Valley. Early records tell of the Wimilchi Indians and Spanish explorers who moved through the area and of a sizeable Mexican land grant, *Laguna de Tache Rancho*, in the vicinity. Fur trappers, sheep herders and wheat ranchers made famous in *The Octopus* by Frank Norris, followed in sequence and finally the orchardists and vineyardists of today. Joseph Draper first settled in 1873 at the site of the city at a spot then known as Kings River Switch on the Southern Pacific Railroad line. A town sprang up known successively as Draperville, Wheatville and finally Kingsburg. Today the town has about 3,843 inhabitants and is well known in the Valley because of the sizeable number of Swedes who have given it a distinctive atmosphere.

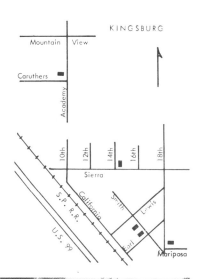

Russell C. Fey

The Hero Home —
1900 14th Avenue
Kingsburg

This handsome frame home, built as a farm house surrounded by fig trees in 1906, was the home of Mr. and Mrs. P.G. Hero. They were both born in Sweden where Mr. Hero began training as a carpenter at the age of fourteen. Emigrating to the United States they settled first in Ishpenning, Michigan, before coming to Kingsburg. Mr. Hero did all the construction work on his house himself and the materials were hauled in a horse drawn lumber wagon from Sanger since there was no lumber yard in Kingsburg at the time.

The house is reminiscent of the Stick Style. Most distinctive features are the compass pattern porthole and the small gable over the front bay window which repeats the design of the main gable.

Mr. Hero died of a stroke during the great flu epidemic of 1918, and the funeral was held under a fig tree in the yard with everyone in attendance wearing flu masks. In 1938, the property was purchased by Frank Rosander who refurbished the home and completely landscaped the yard. The mature trees and garden make this a most distinctive property in the section still known as Hero's Addition.

The N.M. Johnson Home
1355 Smith Street
Kingsburg

In 1908 a local Kingsburg jeweler, N.M. Johnson, contracted with a builder from the east, a Mr. Hedberg, to construct this large, three story frame home. It features a very simple facade which contrasts with some very fancy stickwork in the peak of the gable. The large basement was dug by Mr. Johnson, and all the dirt was hauled out in a wheelbarrow. Mrs. Lucy Johnson, wife of the builder, still resides in the home.

Russell C. Fey

Russell C. Fey

Swedish Methodist Church
1301 Smith Street
Kingsburg

This two-story frame house was built in 1908 as a parsonage of the Swedish Methodist Church. It features a wide curving brick veranda across the front and two attractive leaded glass panels. Other features include a hip roof with the gable placed to one side of the structure and shingled cornice returns. When the Swedish Methodist Church merged with another Methodist Church in town, the house was sold to the Catholic Church for use as a rectory. In sixty-seven years this house has always been owned and used by a church.

Russell C. Fey

The Johnson Home — 12401 South Academy Kingsburg

This very large two-story clapboard farmhouse located on forty acres of land is a point of interest on South Academy Avenue. It was built by Solomon Johnson in 1906. There are many sharp contrasts of architectural style in the residence. The double roof of the rounded tower is an unusual architectural feature. The four heavy Ionic columns on the porch were originally made for Selma High School but proved to be the wrong size, so they were incorporated into the design of this house. Bay windows on both the first and second floors, and a fine brick chimney are outstanding features of this remodeled and well-maintained home.

Russell C. Fey

The Peterson Home — 1300 18th Avenue
Kingsburg

Erick and Axelina Peterson acquired the twenty acre parcel on which this home was built in 1887. In 1903 this house was built for them by a contractor, Emmanuel Benson. The house passed through numerous ownerships and in the 1930's was owned by a life insurance agent, Julian Jacobson, who raised and trained purebred Arabian horses on the property as a hobby. The house was converted into a duplex in 1953. Two years ago it was purchased by Kingsburg city councilman Albert Hovnanian and his wife, and they are restoring it to its original condition. The attractive front door with oval glass, the sunburst detail in the pediment and the stained glass panel over the front window are details which will enhance the completed restoration.

Reedley

Reedley, with its population of about 8,131, is a representative town of the Valley. When irrigation water and a railway came through the area, a town named after a large rancher, Thomas Law Reed, appeared. Because of its leisurely growth, a number of homes older than most of those in Fresno, have survived to provide a revealing glimpse of the 1880's and 1890's. Where Reedley now stands, Wet-chi-whet Indians once roamed and early descriptions refer to waving acres of wild oats, bands of elk and myriads of duck which thrived in the Kings River and nearby sloughs. Later, huge stock ranches, followed by equally large wheat ranches and finally the characteristically smaller plots of today, green with citrus groves and vineyards, became the typical scene.

The influx of a large number of Volga Germans has given a distinctive cast to this pleasant community with its schools and Mennonite churches.

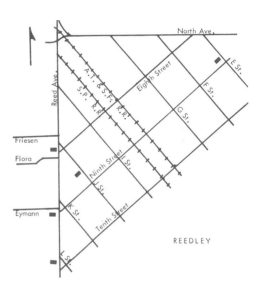

Russell C. Fey

The Besaw Home — 857 E Street Reedley

In 1905 the Besaw family built this eight room home on a colony lot purchased for $500. James L. Besaw designed and built the house using cobble rock brought from the Kings River for his foundation. A square shaped tower, an unusual form, with a stained glass window surmounts a porch roof with extreme curvilinear design. Wood stoves provided heat for the big home.

The property is now owned by the Albert Parachians whose shoe repair store grew into a men's shoe store.

The Back Home —
935 J Street
Reedley

Russell C. Fey

Perhaps the most strikingly unusual design of all the homes from the Reedley area in this book, is the stylish two story house built by Arthur Back in 1905. Mr. Back was one of a group of Finns attracted to the Reedley area by Baron Aksel Wahren, a Finnish nobleman and trained agronomist who had been exiled from Czarist Russia. Impressed by the fertile soil of this area he urged the Finnish people by pamphlet and speeches to settle here. A group of farm enthusiasts in San Francisco who dreamed of a Finnish Colony in America took his advice. One of these was Mr. Back who in company with the other like-minded men first investigated on Thanksgiving Day in 1904 and then settled in Reedley.

Mr. Back bought a town lot on J Street where he built this harmoniously designed home. He had been apprenticed in carpentry in New York and knew how to build well. Hence his home, probably the first Finnish residence in the San Joaquin Valley, stands out today as an example of sound, lasting construction. He copied a type of dwelling familiar to him, one similar to a Finnish Railroad Master's home. With its steeply pitched roof and the curved and shingled barge-boards which mark out impressive U shaped gables, the dwelling must have provided a warm reminder of homeland for the many Finnish people who found the residence a friendly stopping place on their way to their new homes. The interior is done in natural pine woodwork. The house today is commonly known as the Beck Finnish home. The name is probably of Swedish origin and was properly written with an umlaut over the "a."

When Baron Wahren was permitted to return to Finland, Back became a land agent and continued the publicity program among Finnish-Americans. He advertised and traveled widely, on one occasion going as far north as Astoria and Portland, Oregon. As a result of that trip, several families moved south. They were sent by Back to the west of the Kings River near the Parlier district, where there was a large level acreage but no irrigation ditches. For a time this was the largest Finnish settlement in the region.

It is reported that on the fiftieth anniversary of Finnish Pioneers in Reedley held in May, 1955, "that there were in the area 133 Finnish-born residents, 332 first generation American-born citizens, and 465 second generation descendants."

96

The J.J. Eymann Home — 295 South Reed Avenue
Reedley

This house at 295 South Reed Avenue was built for Daniel T. Eymann shortly after his arrival in Reedley in October, 1903 but when Mr. Eymann was accidentally killed in 1911 his son, J.J. Eymann, acquired the home, and it is commonly referred to as the J.J. Eymann home. The background of this house and the August C. Eymann home which is also discussed in the following page provide a good example of the settlement and development of Reedley.

Daniel T. Eymann was a well-to-do Kansas farmer who moved with some of his livestock, farm equipment and household goods, to southern California near Upland. Here he purchased an orange grove, but decided that the land was too high priced. A Santa Fe Railroad land agent extolled the merits of the Reedley area and Mr. Eymann with his wife and smaller children and his son, August C. Eymann and family settled in Reedley.

The Eymanns were the first Mennonites to come to Reedley and subsequently Mr. Eymann traveled to the Middle West and East urging other Mennonites to take up land here where they could be among their own. His missionary enterprise was an important factor in the establishment of the well known Mennonite community in the Reedley vicinity.

Plans for the large home had been purchased from owners of a similar home in Upland. Most distinctive features are the wrap-around porch and the various types of windows which provide interesting variations. Fish scale shingles in the gables, a sloping wall finished in shingles at the second story level and the clapboard siding make interesting variations of texture. Features of the interior include stained glass windows, carved newell posts and a solid oak fireplace with a small oval mirror.

J.J. Eymann became the first mayor of Reedley.

The Bauder Home — 109 South Reed, Reedley

Russell C. Fey

Reedley's first marriage took place in this wood frame home in 1890 when Lela A. Bauder, daughter of the Reverend T.J. Bauder for whom the house had been constructed the previous year, became the bride of Daniel Lyle Reed, nephew of T.L. Reed for whom the town of Reedley was named. The house was the first home built on a colony lot. In 1888 when it was begun only one other building existed in the wheat field which had been bought from F.M.V. Merritt, an original stockholder in The 76 Land and Water Company. The Bauder family lived in one side of their barn while the house was under construction.

Reverend Bauder had moved to the Reedley area from Selma in order to help found the United Brethren Church. On November 17, 1888 he was elected a church trustee by the Quarterly Conference of the United Brethren Church and subsequently played a significant part in raising money for the church. He was one of the early ministers of the church.

The A. C. Eymann Home
417 South Reed, Reedley

This pleasing and spacious home was built by Daniel T. Eymann for his son, August Eymann and his family in 1904. Architect C.B. Shaw planned this hip roofed house with five gables and the deep porch with curving roof around two sides. Carpenters Cornelius Shraeder and Edward Corlett are said to have received $1,000 for their labor.

The bay window protruding under the porch roof is unusual for this period. Clapboard sides, fish scale gable shingles, a front door flanked by narrow windows, are all familiar features of Valley construction of the period. The sturdy, well proportioned home symbolizes very nicely the orderly and constructive lives of the Eymann family in the Valley.

The Eymanns were a numerous family, founders along with other German-speaking families of the Mennonite church in Reedley, civic leaders and prominent businessmen in the Valley. Eventually there were in this residential area five Eymann homes, which the neighbors sometimes referred to as the Eymann Colony.

Courtesy Elsie Brewer

Sanger

Sanger, a pleasant town of about 10,000 inhabitants was named for Joseph Sanger, Jr. of the Pacific Improvement Company, the land holding company of the Southern Pacific Railroad. Until 1889 Centerville, a stage coach station on the Kings River had been the most important town in the south central portion of Fresno County but with the coming of the railroad population shifted to the newly founded town. At first the economy of Sanger rested on lumber brought from the mountains on the "longest flume in the world" and on wheat from the surrounding fields. In fashion characteristic of the Valley, however, citrus crops, grapes and cotton came in. Today frozen food plants and packing plants which line the railroad tracks attest the importance of Valley agri-business.

Courtesy Marjorie Moglia

The Rheingans Home
1390 South Highland Avenue
Sanger

Five generations of the Rheingans family have lived in this ranch house at 1390 South Highland Street near the town of Sanger. The residence, shown here in an old picture taken shortly after its completion, was constructed along with barn and tankhouse in 1904 at a total cost of about $3,000 for Robert V. Rheingans.

The Rheingans family had been one of a group of German farmers who moved west from Wisconsin and became grain growers in what is now downtown Los Angeles in the 1880's. When homes and office buildings of the expanding city threatened the farming operation, Mr. Rheingans moved north to the Sanger area. Drivers, horses, wagons and farm equipment made the nine-day trek over Tehachapi Pass to the San Joaquin Valley. Members of the family came later by train. In Sanger Mr. Rheingans purchased 160 acres, leased 1100 acres and resumed raising wheat, barley and oats. About 1914 the Rheingans turned to grapes and tree fruit, reducing the size of the ranch to 280 acres. Members of the family remembered that, when they began to irrigate, the water table lay only seven to nine feet below the surface.

The two-story frame house is representative of the early homes of many farming families. Wide porches on the west and north sides provided shelter from the hot valley summers, a feature much appreciated in years before the surrounding trees and vines had matured. The porches are supported by turned posts, and the balustrades are of an interesting open design. Simulated brackets can be seen under the eaves of the roof and the porch roof. The frieze boards under the porch repeat the design of the frieze under the roof.

Five generations of the Rheingans family have lived in the house. The present occupant is Skye Rheingans Hannigan, who lives there with her husband Michael and their children. The children are the great-great-grandchildren of the original owner, Robert V. Rheingans.

The Gerner Home — 7659 East Jensen Avenue
Sanger

The John Gerner home at 7659 East Jensen Avenue with its full basement, basic salt box design, clapboard sides, fish scale decorations in the pediment, plus the elaborate barge board and finally the long deep porch are reminiscent of Midwestern homes. The resemblance is not accidental. John Gerner came from Wisconsin in 1890 to farm the eighty acres. When he built his home in 1903, he used as a model houses he had known as a young man in Wisconsin.

When Mr. and Mrs. John Gerner were killed in a tragic auto-train accident, a son, Anson Gerner, took over the home and lived there with his family for fifty-two years.

Both Anson and his wife Sophia were raised and attended schools in Sanger. Mr. Gerner graduated from the University of California and was chief engineer and manager of the Fresno Irrigation District. Mrs. Gerner was for many years a Sanger teacher until her retirement in 1947.

Mrs. Gerner is the granddaughter of two of the founding families of the Sanger area. Her grandfather, William Hazelton, built the first settlement on the Kings River. With Jess Morrow and Harvey Akers he dug the first irrigation ditch from the Kings. Her mother was Mary Jane Akers. The Akers came to the area very early by covered wagon.

Mrs. Gerner's parents moved into town in 1904 so the children could attend school. Their home was located where the Sanger Civic Center is today.

In 1972 both Anson Gerner and his son Anson, Jr. died, and the ranch has since been managed by a daughter-in-law.

Selma

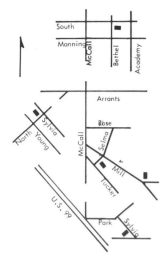

"As far as eye can see are vast bands of wild horses and antelopes," wrote the United States surveyors when they platted the area where Selma now stands. The railroad and water from irrigation canals transformed the area, as with the rest of the Valley, and today Selma with a population of about 7,459 lies among verdant orchards and fields. The townsite was laid out along the Central Pacific line. Then the Centerville-Kingsburg canal passed through the little town encouraging the Frey Brothers, natives of Switzerland, to establish a water powered flour mill in 1877. Other enterprising settlers followed. The light, sandy loam soil proved to be especially good for peaches, and city boosters proudly advertised "Selma, the Home of the Peach." Today both fruit and raisins are processed here.

More than one story concerning the origins of the attractive name, Selma, is current. An article in the *Fresno Bee*, April 3, 1949 holds that the town was named for Selma Michelson Kingsbury whose husband was an official of the Central Pacific Railroad.

Courtesy Selma Museum and Historical Society

The Dusy Home — 1628 Mill Street   *Selma*

This neat and well kept house at 1628 Mill Street at the corner of Mill and Keith Streets in Selma was from 1897 to 1899 the home of Frank Dusy, one of Fresno County's best known pioneers. Although the exact date of construction cannot be determined, a search of the records indicates the probable date to be between 1886 and 1892. W.S. Glines purchased this home in 1905 from Frank Dusy, Jr.

Only two minor changes have been made to the structure. A detached kitchen from behind the house was removed, and a stable on the two lots to the east of the house was torn down and replaced by a garage.

This excellently preserved early Selma home is small in comparison to many of the homes built in this neighborhood. It has three bedrooms, living room, sitting room, kitchen and bath.

The structure is not easy to identify as to overall style, although an Eastlake influence is noted in the gable, eave brackets and porch column capitals. The classical cornices under the eaves, however, recall the Neo-Colonial style. The visible windows are distinctive with the treatment of the flat arch head trim which varies from the typical straight topped windows.

The Staley Home — 1827 Sylvia Street
Selma

The home at 1827 Sylvia Street remains one of the outstanding homes in Selma's first residential area, Whitson's Addition. In 1887, J.E. Whitson, one of the founders of the City of Selma, subdivided the land west of the Southern Pacific Railroad, including the lots on which this two story Victorian home was built.

Ten years later in 1897, Mr. and Mrs. W.S. Staley, who had lived in the Selma area since 1877, purchased the home from Mr. and Mrs. E.E. Bush and Mr. and Mrs. J.O. Baxter. At the time, Mr. Staley was serving as Selma's postmaster. Title passed to the Staley's three daughters, Harriette, Grace and Edith, who lived in and maintained the residence until 1944 when the property was sold. The home, one of Selma's oldest still in good repair, has not been altered and retains its nineteenth century charm.

Architecturally, it is a very simple interpretation of the second empire Victorian house. The second story is not as high as the typical house utilizing the mansard roof, and seems to have a slope which is quite a bit lower than normal. The window coping on the tower differs from that used on the roof molds of the dormers which is unusual. The eaves are supported by a continuously involuted cornice rather than by the typical bracketed cornice with ornately carved brackets. The offset porch stairway without a column at each side is an obvious deviation from the normal symmetry used to enhance and bring attention to the entrance to the house.

102

The Jensen Home — 8262 South Bethel Avenue
Selma

Mr. and Mrs. Christen Jensen built a home at 8262 South Bethel Avenue just at the turn of the century. It was selected for this book because it is one of the large farm homes erected in the 1890-1910 period.

This structure is not an easy one to identify as to overall style influence. However, it has many unusual features of design. The big porch has ornately carved, offset barge boards at the gables. The bay front, contrary to custom, is carried just to the bottom of the second floor instead of to the roof line. The corner gingerbread and brackets accentuate. the change from bay front to squared corners. Another feature is the tank house roof which uses a combination peaked hip roof with large gable dorms protruding.

Other buildings on the property include the barns, implement shed, a tank house whose first two floors housed the hired men and a tenant house.

In 1918 Mr. Jensen retired. He deeded his property to his daughter, Mrs. Clara Sorensen. She still owns the house and keeps it in good repair.

Courtesy Selma Museum and Historical Society

The Vincent Home — 2202 Selma Street
Selma

In May 1904 Manuel Vincent who arrived in Selma from the Azores in 1878 purchased four lots in Frey's Addition to Selma, one block from the business district at the corner on Selma and Mill Streets. There he built this large home of predominantly Queen Anne Style, distinguished by the polygonal turret at the front corner of the house. A differentiation of wall finishes is displayed by the change from wide shiplap siding on the first floor to a much narrower style on the second floor. The shape of the bay window under each main gable indicates the irregularity of the plan, again typical of Queen Anne Style.

Vincent, who was a blacksmith and later had a buggy shop, became president of the First National Bank of Selma. Selma was incorporated in 1893 and the name M. Vincent appears on the incorporation papers. Both he and his son, Paul, served as Mayor.

Old-timers tell of the fashionable parties held in the house and the Vincent girls were known for their beauty and charm.

In 1928 the Paul Vincent family moved into the house and lived there until 1945 when it was sold to Sam Apple. In 1974 the City of Selma purchased the property for the future city hall site. The Selma Historical Museum Society plans to move this home to its Pioneer Village.

Called "the most unusual house" in Selma, the stone house at 2128 North Street is almost completely built of cobblestones. Located on the corner of Grant and North Streets, this dwelling is the last existing private residence in the business block.

Dr. T.A. Booker had planned to build a house of stones when Truman Hart, Mayor of Fresno, called him one day. Mayor Hart told him that there were several carloads of rocks available. The doctor purchased thirty-five tons of the cobblestones and had them delivered to Selma from Friant. Dr. and Mrs. Booker designed the building and supervised its construction. They moved into their creation on July 4, 1919.

Dr. Booker was to live in his "dream house" for only thirteen months when he passed away. Mrs. Booker continued to live in and maintain the home until her death in 1973.

In plan, form and elevation this house would generally be classified as a Bungalow, or more properly Bungaloid (because of the second story) — both of which are more definitive terms to describe plan type rather than total architectural style. The hipped roof rather than a gable roof over the porch marks a deviation from the usual design theme of the Bungalow.

The use of straight stick brackets to support the eaves at the gables is reminiscent of the Western Stick Style, which was the principal style used in the Bungalow or Bungaloid plan type. The cobblestone influence on the Bungalow was derived early in the development of the style by the Greene Brothers who introduced its use for fireplaces and chimney construction. Here we see the cobblestones on the whole lower floor and the chimney with the upper story surfaced in horizontal boards. The combination is an interesting one, providing visual contrast.

The Booker Home — 2128 North Street
Selma

The Vincent Home

continued from page 52

establish Jefferson School at the corner of Fowler and Shaw Avenues. A modern Jefferson School stands at this location today.

After selling most of their rural holdings, the Vincents moved to 221 Blackstone Avenue in 1888 and actively participated in civic affairs. Elected to the State Assembly in 1887, he became a close associate of Mr. Wright in drafting and enacting the famous Wright Irrigation Law. He served as County Assessor for four years, president of the Y.M.C.A., promoter and director of the horse-drawn streetcar line and trustee of the city schools.

About 1903 the Vincents bought twenty acres on Bloomington Avenue (now San Pablo) and sub-divided it as the Markley-Vincent Tract.

Mr. Vincent listed himself as a "capitalist" in the city directory, with investments in mining and oil. He became president of the Confidence Oil Company in Coalinga and president of the Fresno Pine Ridge Railway.

Joseph Vincent died in 1910. His widow, their daughter, Flora, and her husband, Charles T. Elliott, continued living in the home. Mr. Elliott was Deputy County Assessor for twenty years and a grammar school principal for ten years. In 1951 Mrs. Elliott died, the last family member to occupy the home.

Certainly Joseph P. Vincent personified the pioneer spirit of many early Fresnans. He was a young man of vision and enthusiasm who saw beyond the raw desert land to its unlimited opportunities.

The Thompson Home

continued from page 55

touched my life . . . I did the tapestry as if I were doing it for myself and if the person had not wanted it . . . I would gladly have kept it. So far no one has suggested that I keep one."

Following a 1935 exhibit of most of the twenty-two tapestries she had completed in the previous twenty years, Marguerite explained that "the tapestry paintings are very good things for an artist to do who has children to take care of. You see painting is continuous and more fluid than this sort of thing . . . This can be picked up and put down at will . . . It never used to hurt my eyes either, but I'm afraid it does a little now. I shan't do any more of

them. I am appalled at the thought of the work that went into these things . . . "

The children she spoke of, born in 1915 and 1917, have carefully preserved their famous parents' studio, correspondence and remaining works. Several contributions to the Fresno Arts Center's permanent collection have been made by Mr. Tessim Zorach and his sister, Dahlov Zorach Ipcar.

After years of concentration on embroidery, Marguerite returned to painting and she exhibited regularly until her death in 1968, although these later paintings never received the critical acclaim accorded the tapestries.

Despite the earlier promise not to embroider another, the charming depiction of Marguerite and her sister, entitled "My Home in Fresno" was completed in 1949. Perhaps this tapestry is the one Marguerite finally made for herself. In retrospect, the childhood years in the quiet valley town may have seemed important to remember.

The Jamieson Home

continued from page 90

southeast corner a bedroom opens on the screened porch, and at the opposite end the porch is divided into a pantry opening into the kitchen, and a "Chinaman's room". Every early ranch had a Chinese cook to serve the needs of the family and the crew of hired men.

In the kitchen a big wood-burning range on the north wall connected with a brick chimney which also served the living room's cast iron heating stove. The range had iron coils in the firebox to heat water for a storage tank which sat on an elaborately molded cast iron support. The sink, with its hot and cold running water, had painted wooden drainboards.

Surrounded by gardens, the house commands a splendid view to the east of distant orchards and vineyards, the dull gold foothills and the Sawtooth Range of the High Sierra.

In 1915 Pearl Edgerly, whose family had developed 200 acres in the Gould Colony where Ratcliffe Stadium now stands, married Alfred Smith and went to live on the ranch near Fowler. A 1913 graduate of the University of California, she became a charter member of the Fresno Branch of the American Association of University Women when it was organized in 1916. Mrs. Smith still lives on the ranch.

In Memoriam

These homes from the original research list have fallen victim to fire and the bulldozer since our study began.

175 N. Clark

This residence of Mr. and Mrs. Albert Downing Olney was constructed in 1891. Mr. Olney operated the Olney and Jonsen Boot and Shoe Shop on Mariposa for many years. A daughter Bernice was chairman of the English Department at Fresno High School and her sister Ruby was society editor of the old *Fresno Republican*. Albert Clyde Olney, a son, was principal of Fresno High School, president of Marin County Junior College and State Superintendent of Secondary Education. Ruby and Bernice lived in the home until 1967. Rollin Pickford's watercolor of this home is reproduced on the cover of this book.

935 T Street

William Dyer Noble came to Fresno in 1889 and with his brother, G.B. Noble, was connected with fruit packing almost from the inception of the industry. Their Eagle Packing Company was located first in Central California Colony and later in the city. A daughter, Dorothy Noble Hill, served as society editor of the *Fresno Bee*. This home was built by W. D. Noble in 1894.

In 1897 the *Fresno Republican* published a promotional book called *Imperial Fresno*, which featured photos of many early Fresno homes, ranches and businesses. Until it was torn down by the Redevelopment Agency in 1974, the Noble house was the last house in the city still standing that had been featured in this book.

929 T Street

J.H. Zieske, a dispatcher for the Santa Fe Railroad, constructed this house in 1900. On his death in 1932, it was acquired by his daughter and son-in-law, Mr. and Mrs. Gail Hare, who lived there until it was torn down in 1974 by the Redevelopment Agency. Mr. Hare was a rancher. His parents were Dr. George Hare and Dr. Jessie Hare, a famous team of physicians who came to Fresno in 1891 and established the Hare Sanitarium. It contained the first operating room and facilities for taking the first X-ray pictures in the san Joaquin Valley. In 1895 they established the first accredited nurses' training program in Fresno.

Las Palmas

Fresno County ranks first among California's wine growing centers. One of the pioneers of this industry was Benjamin R. Woodworth, grandson of the author of "The Old Oaken Bucket," who bought land in the Nevada Colony in 1890 and planted 160 acres of grapes and a large pear orchard. *Imperial Fresno*, published in 1897, described an idyllic country villa "nestled in a grove of tropical trees and shrubs of every variety" and approached by two palm-lined drives. By this date, the vineyard was owned by the English firm, Balfour-Guthrie Investment Company, and managed by Hector Burness. The original home was replaced with a later structure which burned down within the last three months as the property was being readied for development as an industrial park.

Glossary

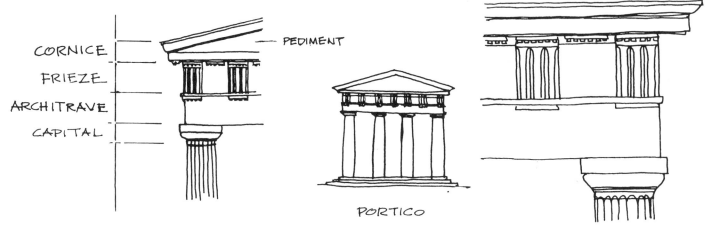

CORNICE
FRIEZE
ARCHITRAVE
CAPITAL

PEDIMENT

PORTICO

CLASSIC ORDERS

ENTABLATURE

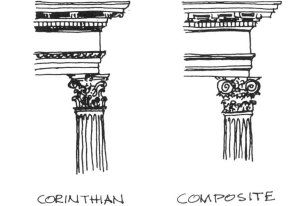
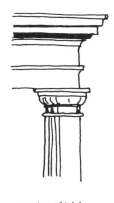

GREEK DORIC   IONIC   CORINTHIAN   COMPOSITE   TUSCAN

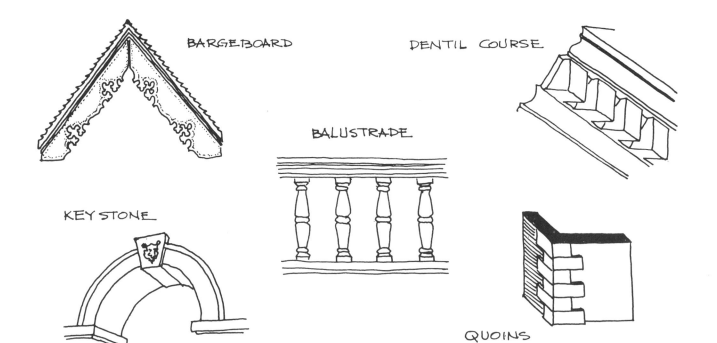

BARGEBOARD   DENTIL COURSE

BALUSTRADE

KEY STONE

QUOINS

Glossary

ARCHITRAVE. The lowest of the three main parts of an entablature; more loosely, the molded frame surrounding a door or window.

BALUSTRADE. A series of short posts resting on a base and supporting a continuous horizontal member.

BARGEBOARD. A strip of wood placed under the edge of a gable and often decorated with jigsaw designs.

BATTEN. As discussed here, a strip of wood usually two to four inches wide and eight to twelve feet long which was nailed over the joint of parallel boards; a device to hold them together and to seal an outside wall.

BAROQUE. A term to describe an exaggerated or florid style of late Renaissance architecture; irregularly shaped.

BAY WINDOW. A window projecting from one side of a building allowing more light into the interior. Sides of the projection may slant out at an angle to the building or join the building at "squared" right angles.

BOND. In masonry the overlapping of joints in successive courses.

BUNGALOW. Small single-story house most characteristically in Western Stick Style with two broad gables to the front, the gable of a porch-veranda in front being echoed by that of the body of the house behind and to one side. Bungaloid is very similar but has a second story.

BRACKET. A projecting support.

CANTILEVER. A bracket which supports a balcony.

CAPITAL. The head or crowning feature of a column.

CLAPBOARD. Overlapping horizontal boards forming an outside wall.

CLASSICAL REVIVAL STYLE (Neo-Classical). Very similar to Greek Revival Style. Buildings were generally larger than those in the Greek Revival Style and simpler in effect. A style that received impetus from the Columbian Exposition and flourished in the early 1900's.

COLONNADE. A series of columns placed at regular intervals and supporting an entablature.

CORINTHIAN. One of the Greek and Roman orders having a fluted shaft, a capital decorated with acanthus leaves and spirals on the upper corners.

CORNICE. The upper projecting portion of an entablature, or any projecting molding along the top of a building, finishing or crowning it.

DENTIL. Small square blocks, resembling a row of teeth, used in a row or course.

DORIC. The earliest order of Greek architecture and with a simple capital.

DORMER. A window framed and roofed like a miniature house which projects from the roof.

EASTLAKE STYLE. Named after Charles Eastlake, English author of *Hints on Household Taste* and furniture designer—characterized by bevelled edges, and incised designs, often combined with "strip" or Stick Style architecture.

ENTABLATURE. The upper part of an order, consisting of architrave, frieze and cornice.

FACADE. The front or face of a building.

FAN LIGHT. A semi-circular or semi-elliptical window above a door.

FINIAL. The carved or molded ornament crowning a gable or spire.

FISH SCALE DESIGN. A pattern of shingles rounded on exposed extremity. Sometimes referred to as "scalloped."

FRENCH RENAISSANCE. Chateau de Chenonceaux in France, which provided inspiration for the Kearney Mansion, offers an example. It had a strikingly irregular skyline, sharply pitched roofs, large dormers, and graceful turrets corbeled out from the building. The total plan was massive, but there was much ornamentation inspired by Italian and Classical examples.

FRIEZE. A horizontal band between the architrave and cornice.

GABLE. The triangle of wall surface formed by the meeting of two sloping roof lines at the end of a ridged roof. Gablet is a small gable, for example, over a dormer window.

GEORGIAN COLONIAL STYLE. A style that flourished in the eighteenth century, characterized by a symmetrical facade and raised first floor with a course of brick surrounding.

GEORGIAN REVIVAL STYLE. Rectangular in plan with a minimum of minor projections and with strictly symmetrical facades. Roofs are hipped, double pitched, or of gambrel form; eaves detailed as classical cornices. Roof often topped with a flat deck with a surrounding railing or balustrade; sometimes there is a central cupola.

GINGERBREAD. Pierced curvilinear ornament, executed with the jigsaw or scroll saw, under the eaves of roofs.

GOTHIC STYLE. Characterized in American revival by high, pointed houses with peaked roof, pointed arches, and trimmed with gingerbread.

GREEK REVIVAL. Derived from the Greek temple with a portico across the entire front and roof ridge running from front to back. Roofs were low pitched or flat; no arches; lintels and beams over windows and doors. Wooden buildings were invariably painted white. Similar to Jeffersonian Classical Style and Neo-Classical Style.

HEADER BRICK. Brick laid in a wall so that its shorter ends are exposed.

HIPPED ROOF. A roof whose external angle is formed by the meeting of two sloping surfaces.

IONIC. One of the three orders of Greek and Roman architecture characterized by the two lateral volutes of the capital.

continued

ITALIANATE. Term for a period deriving its forms and ornament from 15th and 16th century Italian architecture (i.e. bell towers and villas of Italy) and characterized by cube-shaped construction, tall narrow windows and doors, angled bay windows a small portico with classic columns, and a flat, heavily bracketed roof line.

ITALIAN VILLA. A variation of the Italianate, but larger with an entrance through a tower facade leading into a central hall with flanking rooms.

JEFFERSONIAN CLASSICAL STYLE. Derived from the Roman temple; buildings characterized by use of columns; generally square and massive appearance; low roof line. Frequently found features included semicircular windows in the pediment; straight topped windows. Flourished in the late 18th century and early 1800's. Similar to the Greek Revival and Neo-Classical Styles.

LOGGIA. A gallery or arcade having one or more of its sides open to the air.

MANSARD. A roof with a double pitch, the lower slope being steeper than the upper slope.

MISSION STYLE. Characterized by semi-circular, sometimes segmental arches; tiled roofs which are usually hipped; gables of curvilinear design; balconies are frequent; no sculptural ornament.

MOLDING. Continuous projections or incisions used as a decorative band.

NEWEL OR NEWEL POST. The principal post at the top or bottom of a flight of stairs, supporting the handrail.

PALLADIAN WINDOW. A window in the form of a round headed archway with a narrower compartment on each side.

PEDIMENT. A triangular space at the end of a low-pitched gabled roof.

PILASTER. A rectangular column projecting only slightly from a wall.

PRAIRIE STYLE. Usually two-story houses with wings which may open up into porches at their extremities. Emphasis is on the horizontal; gently sloping roofs; low proportions, ribbon windows, dark wood stripping may continue the sill line around the house. Parapets of porches, steps and balconies strongly defined by projecting caps or copings.

QUEEN ANNE. A popular late Victorian style characterized by a variety of unusual chimneys, spindled verandas, high peaked roofs, stained glass windows, shingles and corner towers (round, square or octagonal). Ornamental combinations were endless and the style was often termed "hodge-podge."

SOFFITT: The under horizontal face of an architrave or or overhanging cornice.

STICK STYLE. A late 19th century architectural style whose design elements evolved from balloon frame construction techniques. It was characterized by tall proportions, irregular silhouette, projected eaves, diagonal "stickwork" and applied wood (often strips) suggesting unseen structural framing. Western Stick Style is distinguished from Stick Style by more horizontal lines and greater use of shingles.

STRETCHER BRICK. Brick laid in a wall so that the side is exposed.

WAINSCOTING. Wood paneling applied to an internal wall.

VICTORIAN STYLE. There is no consistently identifiable Victorian Style. The term is applied loosely to many dwellings constructed in the post-Civil War period with stylistic features drawn from many sources. Sharply pitched roofs, frequent use of towers and turrets; use of Eastlake detail (gingerbread) and other elaborate ornament are associated with the term. Asymmetrical. Victorian Gothic is a more florid version of the Victorian Style with special emphasis on vertical lines. High Victorian is derived from the work of French architects during the Second Empire and is characterized by the use of the mansard roof and opulent use of wooden ornamentation.

Bibliography

Primary Sources.

Building Permits, Department of Planning and Inspection, Fresno City.

Fresno City and County Directories.

Land Titles, courtesy of Safeco Title Insurance Company.

Births, Marriages and Deaths, Bureau of Vital Statistics, Fresno County.

Oral History Collection, Fresno County Public Library.

Unpublished Letters and Oral Interviews. Collected by the Historic Homes Committee, Fresno Branch, American Association of University Women.

Newspapers, Pamphlets and Maps.

Fresno Bee.

Fresno Republican.

Fresno Weekly Expositor

Pamphlets, Roy J. Woodward Memorial Library, California State University, Fresno.

Pamphlets and Maps, Fresno County Historical Society.

Books, Articles and Theses.

American Heritage, *An American Heritage Guide to Historic Houses of America Open to the Public.* American Heritage Publishing Company, New York, 1971.

Angel, M., compiler, *A Memorial and Biographical History of the Counties of Fresno, Tulare and Kern, California.* The Lewis Publishing Company, Chicago, 1892.

Davis, Ellis A., *Davis' Commercial Encyclopedia of the Pacific Southwest.* Davis Publishing Company, Oakland, 1915.

Eaton, Edwin, *Vintage Fresno.* Huntington Press, Fresno, Calif., 1965

Elliott, W.W., *History of Fresno County,* Valley Publishers, Fresno, California, 1973; a reprint of edition published by Wallace W. Elliott and Company, San Francisco, 1882.

Fresno County Centennial Committee. *Fresno County Centennial Almanac,* Fresno, 1956.

Imperial Fresno: Resources, Industries and Scenery. Fresno Republican, Fresno, 1897.

McGroarty, John, *Fresno County: The Geographical Hub of the State of California.* Fresno County Expositions Committee, Fresno, California, 1915.

National Collection of Fine Arts, *Marguerite Zorach 1908 to 1920: The Early Years.* Smithsonian Institution Press, City of Washington, 1973.

Nickel, Katherine, compiler, *Beginnings in the Reedley Area, A Treasury of Historical Accounts 'Till 1913.* (privately published), 1961.

Richey, Elinor, *Remain to be Seen, Historic California Houses Open to the Public.* Howell-North Books, Berkeley, California, 1975.

Smith, Wallace, *Garden of the Sun.* (4th ed.) Max Hardison — A-1 Printers, Fresno, California, 1960.

Department of Parks and Recreation, *Procedural Guide, Historic Resources Inventory.* State of California, 1973.

Thickens, Virginia Emily, *Pioneer Colonies of Fresno County.* M.A. Thesis, University of California at Berkeley, 1939.

Thompson, T.H., *Official Historical Atlas Map of Fresno County.* Thompson Publisher, Tulare, California, 1891.

Vandor, Paul, *History of Fresno County,* 2 vols. Historical Record Company, Los Angeles, California, 1919.

Walker, Ben Randal, *Fresno Community Book.* Arthur H. Cawston, Fresno, California, 1946.

Walker, Ben Randal, "1882 to 1885 Fresno County, A Municipality in the Making," *Fresno County Historical Society Publication,* Volume I, Number 2, Fresno, California, 1935.

Walker, Ben Randal, *The Fresno County Blue Book,* Arthur H. Cawston, Fresno, California, 1941.

Whiffen, Marcus, *American Architecture Since 1780, A Guide to the Styles.* The M.I.T. Press, Massachusetts Institute of Technology, Cambridge, Massachusetts and London, England, 1969.

Winchell, Lilbourne, *History of Fresno County and the San Joaquin Valley.* Arthur H. Cawston, Fresno, California, 1933.

Zorach, William, *Art is My Life,* World Publishing Company, 1967.

Index

1904 - A more leisurely pace, a gentler age as Judge Nye enjoys a quiet moment on his spacious veranda near Fowler.

WALNU

1 METHODIST CHURCH
2 CATHOLIC CHURCH
3 STEAM FLOUR MILL
4 COUNTY HOSPITAL
5 COUNTY COURT HOUSE
6 MORROW HOUSE
7 OGLE HOUSE
8 WELLS FARGO EXPRESS
9 POST OFFICE
10 DEXTER LIVERY STABLE

BIRDSEYE VIEW O

Printed & Published

THO S. E.HU

REAL ES